Testimonials

"He has an uncanny gift for turning big money into bigger money for a select group of clients."

—ORANGE COAST MAGAZINE

"Over the past eight years through a variety of investment vehicles from real estate to bonds to special stock funds, I have averaged the equivalent of fully taxed investments at almost 15% (with no down years). I really value the personal service and consistency of returns."

—LARRY S., CHAIRMAN

"His integrity, authenticity and genuine care for those he is in relationships with distinguishes him from many in the financial world. I have come to value his leadership, service and financial acumen."

—JOHN W., PRESIDENT

"Mark is an astute investor and has afforded me fabulous returns on my money. Even in the tenuous markets after September 11, my investments did well. I feel fortunate to be Mark's client, and to feel like I am his friend."

—KATHI B., WIDOW

"It is both refreshing and encouraging to meet a man who daily 'walks the talk.' He is not only a person of exceptional character, but also one whose strength stands up under pressure. I would confidently trust him with my resources and my life."

—JOHN M., PRESIDENT

"Mark is an unusual financial advisor in that he has expertise in a number of different fields including stock and bond portfolio management, real estate investments, venture capital investments and private business investments. This allows Mark to recommend various alternative investment options depending on the current economy and financial markets. I have known Mark for over 10 years and can vouch that he is a man of the highest personal character and integrity."

—DON H., INVESTOR

"Mark embodies the best qualities one could possibly desire in a financial advisor. He demonstrates warmth, caring, excellent professional knowledge of his field and an integrity I trust implicitly. The diversity of my investments mean that despite a highly volatile economic climate, I am protected."

—LINDA M., WIDOW

"He has the keen ability to assess the temperature of the economy and make wise financial decisions. As a result, my portfolio has had significant growth in a non-robust economy. His clients' best interests are his first priority. It has been an honor to know and work with him."

—CHRISTY M., INVESTOR

"I have been a client of Mr. Van Mourick for over 10 years and have found him to be a reliable and trustworthy advisor. He has helped me, as a senior citizen, to maintain a balanced portfolio, which has kept my income stable and my principal secure."

—BEVERLY H., INVESTOR

"You not only do an outstanding job managing our finances, but you do it with style, kindness and complete excellence. We are blessed to have found you to assist us in investing the resources God has entrusted to us."

—BRYE AND SALEM M., INVESTORS

"How refreshing to read something practical, insightful and strategic. High net worth or not, this book speaks to everyone."

—JIM JOHN S., INVESTOR

"During the times when I was feeling a heavy burden with my IRS audit to the time I broke my arm and was unable to work, it always seemed you had developed a financial cushion for me to fall back on. Without your work and direction, Mark, I don't know what I would have done during those times."

—GABE H., INVESTOR

CASH OUT
CASH IN

The After-Success
Investment Guide

Mark Van Mourick

Valuable Lessons from a

Leading Investment Advisor

to the Ultra-Wealthy

CASH OUT, CASH IN by Mark Van Mourick
Published by Creation House Press
A part of Strang Communications Company
600 Rinehart Road
Lake Mary, Florida 32746
www.creationhouse.com

Library of Congress Catalog Card Number: 2003104165
International Standard Book Number: 1-59185-226-9

Second Printing. This book was previously published in October, 2000, by Optivest Press, ISBN 0-9702983-0-7

03 04 05 06 — 9 8 7 6 5 4 3 2
Printed in the United States of America

Dedicated to

Tom Kendall

1915–

Contents

Acknowledgments

This book could not have been written without the help of many individuals over the last year to whom I am greatly indebted. Specifically, the rewriting assistance from John Boal added a humanistic touch and readability to my boring original copy. Likewise, the many hour of editing by Ginger Levin and Karyn Green polished my work into a much better product. John Cole, I thank you for the many revisions you endured, along with your excellent graphic designs. A special thanks to Ron Schultz for coordinating all the players to bring this book together, along with Ray Garza for the cover design. Many thanks to Garfield Langmuir-Logan and Roger Neu for their valuable contributions to this book and the lives of my clients. I also wish to thank the managers of the many successful investments my investors and I have enjoyed: Chuck Bayless, Mike Baynes, Geoff Beaumont, Kim Benjamin, Rich Boureston and Michael Todd, Mary Ann Buchanan, Bob Campbell, Phil Carnahan, Chris Cole, Eric Davidson and Gary Davidson, Larry Dunn, Bary Finch, Richard Ganz, Bob Gold, Dan Harkey, Al Hartman, Mark Hitchcock, Marc Kazarian, Tim McCorack,

Dean McFarlan, Steve McNally, Terry Roussel, Rex Ryan, Rod Scribner, Tom Searles, Bethe Strickland, Tony Thompson, Craig Vallely and Jerry Lynch, John Veard, Mary Worrall and Bart Zandbergen. You made the profits. Thank you. On the home front, I wish to thank my staff at OPTIVEST, especially Barbara Cox who typed, edited, proofed, and reread this book over many hours. But, most of all, I would like to thank the dozens of wonderful investors I have worked with over the past 24 years. They have taught me, through victories and defeats, the valuable lessons I share in this book.

Introduction

ALTHOUGH I'VE BEEN *fortunate to consult and collaborate with scores of successful investors, none has spanned the ages with as much consistent success, with as much savvy decisiveness, or in such a diversified array of investment vehicles as Tom Kendall.*

A superb swimmer, fearless pilot, Caltech instructor, genius inventor with a slew of patents, raconteur and Renaissance man of investments and the world, Tom was brash and brilliant. He was an impatient perfectionist who didn't suffer fools for long. A "long-term contrarian" and maverick visionary, he had an uncanny ability to consistently strike in depressed sectors of various markets—steel, orange groves, oil & gas, and utilities, to name just a few—and sell at enormous profits that made him a multimillionaire. Tom was a committed patriotic citizen who operated by a strict moral code and he was a devoted husband and father. But most of all, he was a man with an unbridled zest for living life to its fullest.

Tom was "extreme" long before anyone else.

While teaching at Caltech during World War II, Tom foresaw the skyrocketing price of steel. So he put his entire life savings as a deposit on three containers of steel for future delivery. While he had no ability to pay for the steel when it was due, he was able to find a buyer before delivery and sold it for a huge profit in the mid-1940s.

With that bankroll under his belt, he started a heating and air conditioning company and developed several new patents along the way. Incredibly efficient as a pioneer with "time and motion" studies, Tom had a keen engineering mind that kept his overhead at a minimum as he perfected his employee output-per-hour charts that helped make his business highly profitable.

In a few short years, Tom had half of the U.S. market for heating and air conditioning units in industrial plants.

This success gave him freedom to fly, literally.

With precise management controls in place and a trusted lieutenant in charge of his thriving business, Tom and two partners bought 13 of those fat PBY planes that land in water, and had three of them outfitted like mobile homes. Taking his young family in tow in the early 1950s, they accompanied him on a year-long, around-the-world journey with a cook, school-teacher, and *Life Magazine* reporter. Despite being shot down over the Red Sea (and then being rescued by the intervention of Greek shipping magnate, Aristotle Onassis), Tom's children still advanced to their next grade level right on schedule.

When they returned to the U.S., Tom's remote but diligent overseeing of his business paid off. He retired his loan on his Inland Valley home in three years, sold his business, and from the 1950s on, never "worked" again in a conventional sense.

But Tom was anything but retired.

Like a sharp-eyed eagle soaring above, searching and searching for his next targeted attack, Tom would spend weeks in his Cessna 310, map in hand, looking for the next under-developed parcel of land to buy. He once saw three cities growing toward one rural area. Naturally he figured that unpopulated area was ripe for future development. So he purchased those acres in the 1960s and reaped a return in the 1980s that was 180 times his initial investment. Another time he used a dirt road as a runway, landed his Cessna and shook on a deal with a farmer for his land, right on the spot.

However, when he focused his attention to investing in the stock market, he would spend weeks doing due diligence on a single public company. Tom once met with the president of a large utility company that was on the verge of bankruptcy. Knowing the government would never let a utility's lights go out, he bought a "boat load" (100,000 shares) at $4 per share. The crisis was averted: The stock went up and 5 years later it was paying a *dividend* of $4 per share! He still owns it today.

Tom's golden touch almost always panned out. He would consistently buy cheap when the market had overreacted to investments with good fundamentals. He successfully bought oil in the early 1970s, stocks in the mid-1970s (after the Dow plummeted 50% from 1972 highs) and bonds (at double-digit yields) in the early 1980s. He planned well, bought low and held on for many years.

My first contact with Tom was as a rookie stockbroker in the late 1970s. He was my best friend's uncle, and he took me under his wing with many late-night sessions regaling this appreciative listener with his numerous successes and quixotic lifestyle.

Then, during the mid-1980s and after I had become Smith Barney's leading retail stockbroker in Orange County, it was Tom who infused me with the energy to spread my wings and open my own investment firm. Thankfully, he also quickly became one of OPTIVEST's first clients, as well as my lifelong mentor.

A blend of Warren Buffet and Indiana Jones, Tom had an amazing ability to know when to rely on his own counsel versus the counsel of his professional advisors. If he felt he knew enough, had done all of his homework, and was up to speed on the sector, he would make the investment decision on his own.

If, however, there was someone more capable of making an investment decision, or if it was out of his expertise, then he would decide before an upcoming meeting that he would take his ego out of the decision-making process and act on that trusted individual's judgment. But he never revealed that it was a *carte blanche* call on the advisor's decision. He always kept that card up his sleeve.

In today's era of instant gratification, Tom's investment philosophy and lifestyle would seemingly be out-of-step. But that's the secret to his lifetime of success.

He didn't follow convention. He charted a course that required more work than most are willing to do: Diversify broadly, do your homework, buy high quality in market segments that are out of current fashion, invest for the long term (decades not just years) and keep enough liquidity to pounce on the opportunities within each succeeding economic crisis.

Then he'd strengthen his knowledge about each of his investments to understand its key elements, follow its seasonal or economic cycle, and rely on experts to manage and oversee the details to each investment.

This carefully crafted path allowed him to build a life around his investment career so he could have time to relax and fully enjoy his flying, skiing, swimming and other passionate pursuits.

Now 88, Tom unfortunately suffers from the debilitating effects of Alzheimer's and resides in a convalescent community.

> To the single, most influential investor in my career—who taught me to trust, encourage and network with those who are experts and leaders in their respective fields; to always make time for yourself and your loved ones; and to live a life of balance—I dedicate this book to my mentor and friend, Tom Kendall.

> Mark Van Mourick
> 2/12/03
> Laguna Niguel, CA

Serious Rock Climbing as the Perfect Metaphor for Serious Investment Planning

STARING UP THE face of vertical rock of El Capitan in Yosemite—a sheer 3,000-foot slab of granite—can be intimidating at first glance: somewhat like staring at a new client's $30 million or $300 million portfolio.

But serious rock climbing is the perfect real-life metaphor for serious investment planning. You must have detailed preparation, acute awareness and intense concentration of all possible risks to get an edge, with every move you make, to reach the proverbial mountaintop.

In preparation for the "El Cap" climb to celebrate my 40th birthday, I had planned diligently and trained extremely hard for two years straight. Besides researching routes and various weather conditions, plotting potential resting ledges, selecting gear, ordering food supplies, studying techniques and expecting the unexpected, I ran hills carrying a backpack full of Diet Coke. In fact, I overtrained for the most challenging ascent of my life.

My partners and I spent six days and five nights climbing a wickedly difficult route up the western face. It demanded 100 percent of our concentration at all times. Dinner was a cold can of chili and a beer to wash it down. Snowing occasionally, gusts of wind howled so fiercely up the mountain that our portaledges at times were levitating in the air.

After mastering all the obstacles, we fulfilled our date with destiny and reached the summit of "El Cap." It was incredibly exhilarating to stand up and celebrate that sweet moment with my partners. Although grueling, I was completely confident throughout the climb and was at peace.

But such a tranquil moment doesn't arrive overnight.

A lover of the rugged outdoors—and one who has always relished the mental and physical challenges of intricate problem-solving—I've had an enormous amount of practice. In high school I formed a rock-climbing club. At the University of Southern California I became president of the Mountaineering Club. I've been a climbing instructor for the Sierra Club and I've extended my passion by teaching climbing to over 1,500 Boy Scouts and kids in youth groups at Joshua Tree National Park, in the desert 140 miles east of Los Angeles.

This exuberance for teaching and leading so many youth has also been the best coping exercise.

After I lost both of my parents in a plane crash at the age of 12, I bounced around several foster homes until I was taken under the wing of my Scout Master. As soon as I turned 18, my boot camp in investing began as I made my first purchases in real estate and the stock market from my parents' inheritance. Thus, unlike most financial advisors, I didn't earn my stripes on the back of a client's portfolio. It was real. It was honest. It was, and still is, producing high returns.

Following graduation from the University of Southern California Business School with dual majors in international finance and management in 1978, I became Smith Barney's leading retail stockbroker in Orange County by 1986. That's when I became well positioned to become an independent financial advisor for my largest clients.

In 1987, I left Smith Barney and cofounded the advisory firm, OPTIVEST. Personally working side-by-side with a select group of clientele and frequently coinvesting in such diverse investments as high tech start-ups, hotels, amusement parks and a chain of Jiffy Lubes, among others, I've also conducted estate-planning seminars with Arthur Anderson and the law firm of Gibson, Dunn and Crutcher.

This seasoned combination of skills that can fully embrace risk-to-reward ratios on every type of investment option is what I bring to the design and palette of future dreams. The stringent discipline of being an accomplished climber has been the ideal foundation for becoming an experienced, proactive and successful financial advisor to some of Southern California's wealthiest families. In addition, I've successfully guided scores of individuals who needed expert advice during each and every step of the way toward selling their multi-million dollar businesses.

In over 24 years as an investment advisor, I have learned what truly leads to success, satisfaction and peace of mind—and what incredibly costly mistakes to avoid—for every type of serious investor. You now have in your hands the "inside scoop" on what normally would have taken dozens of meetings and thousands of dollars in fees to acquire.

Total Risk Management based upon impeccable preparation allows even the most outrageous activity to be conducted with confidence. When I climb, I carefully plan each step, knowing what equipment I will need, and most importantly, anticipating the unexpected.

In fact, 80 percent of the equipment one lugs along is unnecessary if everything goes as expected. You wouldn't need your helmet, rain gear, extra food, first-aid kit or the redundant back-up technical equipment to save you if your primary equipment and techniques couldn't potentially fail you.

Of course, part of risk management is assessing whether you should go at all and knowing when to back off if too many things are going wrong. It's an ongoing process that is part experience, part intuition (sometimes from wrong decisions in the past), part research and part training.

Yet the art and science of risk management takes on a completely new and more critical dimension when you come to the full realization that you do not have a second chance to prepare once you're off the ground.

In investment planning, as in climbing, I've found that Total Risk Management is divided into three primary parts:

1. **Common Sense**—Does it fit your situation? Should you even be in a particular financial vehicle? Maybe it's too risky or perhaps it doesn't help you reach your dream.

2. **Preparation**—Have your financial advisors done due diligence to fully understand the potential risks? Can they sense when to pull back if too many contingencies are going wrong; re-group and live for another day?

3. **Back-Up**—If a serious problem presents itself during the life of a particular financial endeavor, is there a Plan B, Plan C, etc., to safeguard your investment?

Unlike most books that are aimed at the mass financial planning market, this book is for the demanding needs of families with $1 million to $1 billion in assets.

Read straight through or absorbed in sections, it is also intended to be a handy desk guide with its numerous helpful charts and questionnaires. Hopefully, its pages will become dog-eared as you refer back to it often and think through each of the three parts—getting the most out of selling your business, designing a risk-tolerant investment strategy to meet your goals, and then contentedly managing your portfolio efficiently and profitably as a passive investor.

At every stage during the process, I, or the contributors to this book, will point out advantages and disadvantages, pluses and minuses to drive home the need of employing Total Risk Management in your investment portfolio.

By absorbing the counsel of our experienced team of advisors, you will become confident in your actions, knowing how well you have prepared and strategized the optimum route for you, your family and your nonprofit interests; and you will be able to weather any unexpected turn of events (believe me, when there's a bad storm on the mountain, I *know* when to turn back).

But, if you ever decide to elevate your master plan *in person* with our elite corps of financial advisors (or take up the sport of rock or mountain climbing), please don't be a stranger: Simply pick up the phone and give us a call.

While we can't promise you Mt. Everest, we at OPTIVEST will be able to scale any financial mountain you want to climb.

Either way, all the best toward achieving your next dream in life.

Part I

GETTING LIQUID

IF YOU ARE seriously considering—or are in the middle of—"cashing out" a business or real estate asset, this section will help maximize your value.

Maybe it's a business you meticulously built over the years, or perhaps it's a large family real estate holding you inherited. Either way, there are many nuances and details that must be addressed *before* final negotiations.

The first crucial chapter is entitled "Getting the Most From Your Business Sale." It was contributed by Roger L. Neu, Esquire, of Irvine, California, who specializes in mergers and acquisitions for private concerns. Over the last 20 years, Roger has represented both seller and buyer in over 150 business sales or purchases ranging from $5 million to over $100 million. He is a consummate expert in the field and has a website detailing his considerable wealth of knowledge at *www.MandAlawyer.com*.

Next, as I have assisted dozens of CEOs in selling their businesses, I will provide insight on items to review before signing the Letter of Intent. These include specific pre-sale estate planning vehicles, employment agreements with the new owner and how to creatively manage concentrated stock holdings. It is imperative to know your options in advance of accepting a large equity holding. There are ways to "hedge" against potential volatility, borrow on your holdings and get as liquid as you need to realize your dreams.

Chapter 1

Getting the Most From Your Business Sale

by Roger L. Neu, Esquire

D*ON'T LEAVE MILLIONS of dollars on the table because you don't fully understand the process of marketing and selling a business.* There are many common denominators leading to Maximum Value regardless of the type of business you may be selling. They apply across the board whether your business is in aerospace, biotechnology, distribution, engineering, Internet/e-commerce, manufacturing or retail sales.

Maximizing value begins at the moment you're ready to put your life's work on the market. At the close of the day, the right price is a fair price for you and the buyer. The essential point is to insure that you get your "fair price," which if handled correctly, can be a higher price.

VALUATION

Every seller asks, "What is my business worth?" In turn I ask, "What is the maximum a buyer will pay?"

Multinational Company A made an offer to buy a particular business for $35 million. Multinational Company B looked at the same business and offered $60 million. Why the disparity? Each prospective buyer had a different "perception of value." Disparity in perceived value, although not typically this large, occurs everyday in the marketplace.

Another business received an offer for $11 million. That was followed by two comparable offers from other prospective buyers. At the close, after the bidding stopped, the company sold for $16 million.

There may be considerable swings in the value meter during the time a business is on the "For Sale" block. Note that these swings are likely to happen during the sale of your business as well.

A brief overview of how businesses are valued will begin the process of helping you understand how to increase perceived value in your buyer's eyes.

The *bottom line* is that all buyers have to economically justify the purchase price. The buyer arrives at that price by becoming confident in his or her mind that after the acquisition the business will generate sufficient cash flow to provide a reasonable rate of return on the investment.

For example, if a buyer requires a 20% pretax return on investment, that buyer would be willing to pay 5 times the annual cash flow of the business ($100/20 = 5$). A business that generates $2 million per year in cash flow would be valued by that buyer at $10 million ($2 million x 5). The key number, 5, that is used as a multiplying factor of cash flow, is called the Valuation Multiplier.

Depending on the nature of your particular business and the current mindset of the buyer, the Valuation Multiplier can range from 1 (small service company) to infinity (Internet companies with no earnings). After eliminating extremes on both ends, the range of multipliers "generally" sways between 4 and 10. But don't immediately apply this to your business.

Main Factors Affecting the Valuation Multiplier:

1. Financial Performance (past and projected)
2. Management (depth and experience)
3. Market/Product Strength
4. Customer Base
5. Cost Savings from Merging

A "strategic" buyer will generally pay more because a merger within the same industry saves money and adds synergy through consolidation. Larger companies have more resources and may be willing to pay a higher purchase price if there will be a positive effect on their price/earnings ratio.

"Financial" buyers—or investors looking primarily at the rate of return on investment—and smaller purchasers generally will pay less for a business. Additional insight regarding business valuations can be obtained by reading the *Valuation Brochure* at *www.MandAlawyer.com*.

SELECTING A BUSINESS BROKER

Choosing the right business broker is one of the most important decisions you will make in maximizing the value of your business.

A Skilled Business Broker Will:

1. Assist with a preliminary valuation of your business.

2. Help prepare the Selling Memorandum.
3. Provide guidance during negotiations.
4. *Bring qualified buyers to the table.*

Expected Qualities and Characteristics of a Top-Notch Business Broker Include:

1. Working with companies of a similar size.

2. Familiarity with your industry and its key players.

3. A good blend of financial and marketing expertise.

4. Extensive experience in marketing and selling companies.

5. Resources to conduct in-depth market/industry analysis.

6. Extensive database of prospective buyers, including but not limited to investment funds and other institutions.

7. Engaging personality and superior negotiating skills.

Your business broker *must* have high marks in each of these seven categories. A deficiency in any of them will translate into less dollars for your business.

PREPARING THE SELLING MEMORANDUM

It took a lot of ingenuity, hard work, and perseverance to build your business. Now that you have arrived at the point in time that you are ready to sell, you need to be properly rewarded for your efforts. Unfortunately, some business owners believe that prospective buyers should *automatically* appreciate how difficult it was to build the business and how valuable the business really is. This misperception usually leads to one of two results: (1) the Selling Memorandum is too brief; or (2) the Selling Memorandum is lengthy, but contains mostly "fluff" and very little in the way of supporting facts.

When selling a product or service, you probably presented detailed information on how it works, its competitive advantages, etc. Those same marketing techniques must be applied to the sale of your business. The phrase, *You only have one chance to make a good first impression* should be paramount in your mind when preparing the Selling Memorandum.

Maximum Preparation (MP) will result in Maximum Value (MV). Repeat this mantra often, "MP = MV," to achieve your goal.

Preparing the actual Selling Memorandum is often a source of frustration for sellers. Unrealistic expectations can cloud your clarity. It is not a document that can be prepared all the way through by your business broker. It is incumbent upon you, the seller, to provide significant input for the Selling Memorandum. The goal is to have a Selling Memorandum that virtually transports a potential buyer into accepting your Maximum Value. No one can convey the true essence and value of your business better than you can.

While the business broker can give you the framework for the Selling Memorandum, provide in-depth market and industry research, and edit and produce a sharp final product, your keen insight into the potential of your business has to bleed through this key document.

GOING TO MARKET

You selected the ideal business broker and wrote the world's best Selling Memorandum. Now it's show time!

You will receive the greatest value for your business by having the largest number of qualified buyers bidding on your treasured enterprise. The term "qualified" is so important because you can't waste valuable time negotiating with individual buyers—or buyer teams—who do not have the resources or the proper motives to close the deal.

You and your business broker should agree on the marketing approach. If your Selling Memorandum is highly confidential, as it is in many cases, you should pre-approve all recipients of the document. You should not, however, restrict your broker's style of working. Placing too many restrictions upon which potential buyers can be contacted severely limits outside interest.

One common seller's mistake is not allowing the broker to market the business to competitors. This can be a deal-breaker since many privately held businesses are sold to competitors. While prudent precautions should be implemented when providing information to competitors, they generally should be included in the marketing process.

A direct-mail campaign to stimulate interest usually precedes the distribution of the Selling Memorandum. Your business broker then sends the document only to "qualified" buyers who respond to the mailing. Prompt phone follow-up is critical. You never ever want to lose any potential buyers at the front end of the marketing process. Your business broker will not only insure that the appropriate parties receive Selling Memorandums, but also will engage in preliminary negotiations with prospective buyers to ascertain which are the best candidates to buy your business.

Expect this process—preparing the Selling Memorandum, marketing the company, identifying the most likely buyers, and completing the transaction—to take from 3 to 12 months.

FIELDING YOUR SELLING TEAM

Selecting the right business broker is essential. But reaching your Maximum Value can only be obtained if other supporting players on the Selling Team are in place.

Other Selling Team Players Include:

1. CPA
2. Estate Planner
3. Investment Advisor
4. Mergers & Acquisitions Attorney

It is important to establish lines of communication with each of these four players when you begin the marketing process, and certainly before a Letter of Intent is signed. Each of these advisors can not only give specific professional advice, but can also provide valuable business insight into the selling process and final negotiations. Please read the *Team Brochure* at *www.MandAlawyer.com* for additional information on fielding your Selling Team.

Your M&A attorney will be a key player from start to finish in the acquisition process. An experienced M&A attorney can help spot and avoid potential pitfalls as well as guide you safely through the selling process. The M&A attorney provides this

guidance, in part, by helping you quickly and easily understand and resolve issues and obstacles that may come up during
the course of the transaction.

Sellers often ask, "Well, why can't I just use my corporate
attorney to handle the sale?" In return, I ask, "Would you call
your general practitioner if you required delicate brain surgery?"

A sharp M&A attorney is a seasoned specialist who searches
out solutions that not only maximize value, but also assure
you of the successful completion of the transaction. Most
importantly, a skilled M&A attorney can simultaneously deal
quickly and efficiently with minor issues while keeping
everyone focused on resolving major issues. "Majoring in the
minors" will usually drive everyone insane and more often
results in reducing, instead of maximizing, value, and what is
worse—that kind of preoccupation can kill the deal!

Your M&A attorney should be involved at the very beginning of the selling process. He or she should definitely review
the Selling Memorandum before it is mailed, as well as be
involved in the preliminary negotiations before signing the
Letter of Intent. The drafting of the final, bulletproof Letter
of Intent should be the collective expertise of all five of your
advisors.

PERFECTING YOUR LETTER OF INTENT

It's now or never. It's the bottom of the ninth and you've got
to drive in the winning run.

The negotiations leading up to the Letter of Intent (LOI) and
the terms and conditions set forth in the LOI are the most critical stages in achieving Maximum Value. The LOI should
address the price and all the other major terms. Although not
all of the terms are contained in your LOI, as a seller, you

should not assume that the excluded terms can be used as leverage points to increase the purchase price or to change other key terms during negotiations and preparation of the final agreements. Sellers and business brokers who do not take the LOI seriously up front can later find themselves struggling to get to the deal they wanted at the outset.

Even though an LOI may be non-binding, there is a good-faith obligation on both parties to consummate the transaction as set forth in the LOI. Buyers do not look kindly on sellers who try to tweak the LOI. The buyer may terminate the deal or may become confrontational and suspicious because the seller is no longer trusted.

The LOI should address major terms only. The parties must avoid protracted negotiations over minor issues. These will be addressed in the preparation of the final agreements.

Remember that price is only one element. Other factors to weigh include payment terms, security, employment/consulting agreements, lease terms, post-closing liability limits, non-competitive clauses, purchase price allocation, and allocation of deal costs. The terms of sale can be effectively negotiated only if the discussions are undertaken with a thorough understanding of the business, legal, tax, securities and other issues that impact the transaction. Please refer to the *Letter of Intent Brochure* at *www.MandAlawyer.com* for a detailed explanation of the LOI.

USING NEGOTIATION SKILLS TO MAXIMIZE VALUE

The seller's involvement and my involvement in negotiations varies from deal to deal. In some transactions, I have negotiated the entire deal, while other deals have been brought to me after clients have negotiated most of the major terms (performing their own brain surgery).

But Beware: Performing your own brain surgery can be dangerous to your health. Having an experienced business broker and M&A attorney at your side, thoroughly immersing themselves in the transaction, is essential to maximizing your sales price and should always be to your advantage.

Negotiating skills are much more intricate than simply putting on a good show. The parties sitting across from you didn't arrive there by being slouches. They are probably skilled negotiators so just "putting on the Ritz" won't accomplish much. Instead, expert negotiators operate from a point of reference knowing what is the best resolution of each issue. This intuitive skill comes from prior M&A experience and being armed with the facts and legal expertise to support each proposal and each resolution.

For example, if a buyer's position is to make each selling shareholder "jointly and severally" liable for any post-closing liabilities, the attorney needs to know the customary resolution of this issue; i.e., who generally is liable and for what amount, and be able to persuasively present the case for limited liability. This is just one of many imbedded issues that requires prior legal experience and knowledge to help assure you get the best result. This same frame of reference lets the M&A attorney and the business broker know when to press-to-yes, when to say no, when to gently back off issues and which issues are salient to maximizing value and successfully completing the transaction.

Negotiators should have an acute understanding of timing and protocol: when and how quickly to respond, whether to respond verbally or in writing, when to meet or have phone conferences, when to address key terms or negotiating points, and how to time communications and responses to heighten the interest of as many buyers as possible.

Other negotiating skills include knowing whom to meet, what information to provide each level of buyer's management, how to present information clearly and concisely; how to gain the trust of the buyer, and how to read and decipher negotiating techniques.

Additional subtle details in the negotiating process—where to meet, where to sit during a meeting and knowing how to read body language—can all make a difference in this high-stakes game.

Let me illustrate. This example is based on an actual negotiating session in which I was representing the buyer. Eight people sat around the table. There were four on our side and four on the seller's side.

After hours of negotiation, my client, the buyer, offered an increased purchase price that was still *$500,000* less than what he was prepared to pay. A brief pause and some subtle but noticeable body language by the seller and the seller's advisors indicated to me, ever-so-briefly, that they agreed to our offer. After this brief pause, the seller raised some additional objections to the offer. Immediately, I requested a brief adjournment.

Away from the table, I explained to my clients that the brief pause, body language, and other factors suggested that we had met, or were extremely close to meeting, the seller's expectations. At that moment, I recommended that the buyer stand firm (even though they were willing to up the ante another $500,000) and should actually ask for some concessions.

When we reconvened, it became readily apparent that my assessment was correct. Following some additional, but unsuccessful, maneuvering by the seller for a higher price and further negotiations, both the buyer and the seller left satisfied with the deal. Not only did my client save $500,000 in the purchase price, but he also benefited from additional seller concessions worth several hundred thousand dollars.

Bottom Line: The seller lost almost $1 million because of the manner in which he and his advisors handled the negotiations. Don't let this happen to you.

You, the seller, should meet with your business broker and M&A attorney before meeting with buyers or going into these types of negotiating sessions. It is important that each party clearly understands its role and you know what to expect. Sellers should also insist that their advisors be well-armed with the necessary facts before entering negotiations.

The essence of negotiating is understanding and meeting the needs and desires of the buyer. The value of your business increases with each additional benefit you bring to the buyer. Remember the mantra MP = MV (Maximum Preparation = Maximum Value).

Many times the buyer hasn't done the necessary due diligence to fully appreciate the value of your business. Before the negotiations begin, you and your advisors should learn as much information as possible about the prospective buyer or buyers. That information can then be used to present a convincing game plan to show how the buyer will benefit conceptually and financially by acquiring your business.

Additionally, nurturing good relationships between buyer and seller and their respective advisors can enhance each element of the negotiations. Discussions based on respect and integrity are not only more productive, but also more enjoyable. Good relations will benefit you during the transaction and will pay additional dividends as you work with the buyer following the sale.

EMBRACING OTHER VALUE FACTORS

There are also several "nuance"-type factors that must be thoroughly weighed as you step back and examine the big picture of selling your business. Here are eight key points to help enhance the value of your business.

1. **If possible, have audited financial statements available.** Most business brokers concur that audited statements will help increase your purchase price. If an audit is not possible, be certain your financial information is accurately maintained and presented in a professional manner.

2. **Getting paid is important!** The highest price may not be the best offer. Many factors affect value, such as security for future payments; method of payment, i.e. cash, stock or property; contingent payments or performance payments; and future participation in the buyer's business. These factors are described as follows:

   Security—Assurance that deferred payments will be made is essential. If the buyer is a newly formed subsidiary, then the seller should go to the parent company for guarantees and security. In some cases, highly leveraged transactions do not provide any security for deferred payments. If this occurs, the seller needs to step back and carefully weigh this potential red herring to evaluate the real value of the offer.

Stock Payments—Seller beware! If the buyer's stock is accepted as payment, it is usually done as a "tax-free transaction." If you sell the stock soon after the sale, or if the transaction fails to meet the requirements of a "tax-free transaction," your tax benefits disappear.

The defining question is this: Do you want to risk your entire life's work (sales proceeds) on a business (the buyer's business) that you probably have little knowledge of and do not control? Receipt of stock of an established company that is readily traded may have some merit. But, as a rule, sellers and sellers' advisors need to carefully analyze any stock proposal. In a stock transaction, the selling price will usually be higher because of the speculative value of the stock received versus the fixed value of a cash payment or adequately secured note.

Contingent Payments and Performance Payments—Many sellers who have structured their sale with performance payments have second thoughts and generally advise against it. Contingent payments and performance payments are different sides of the same coin: each requires making a portion of the purchase payment contingent upon future performance. Sometimes that performance is dependent on numbers that the seller guarantees to justify the selling price. Sometimes it consists of revenue and/or profit targets that will provide payments to the seller above and beyond the original purchase price.

When payments are based on future performance (as either a guarantee or an incentive),
thorough and careful analysis must be applied to
assure that the seller gets the "value" intended.
This is a mushy area as there are many variables
and financial considerations to evaluate. They
may also be difficult to account for or control.
Future changes in operations and management
could have a major impact on how contingent
payments or performance payments are calculated
and paid. Some other factors to consider include:

- Could your business merge immediately or perhaps later with the buyer's business?

- Could product lines be discontinued, altered or
  changed?

- Could the buyer's method of accounting for overhead and other expenses differ significantly from
  yours?

Contingent or performance payments should
not automatically be excluded, but you must
investigate them with great caution.

Future Participation in Buyer's Business—
Sellers should not focus strictly on the value of
their "business" while overlooking their "individual" value. Added value may be reaped from
finding ways the seller can participate in the
buyer's business. The seller can negotiate significant financial incentives—on top of the purchase

price—to expand or otherwise contribute to the buyer's business after the sale. This is a lucrative opportunity that is often not explored.

3. **Listen to the market and execute precise timing.** Sometimes sellers miss their best deal because it is not the deal they want, only to settle later for a lower offer. If knowledgeable buyers have evaluated your business and negotiations have resulted in final offers, it's likely these offers reflect the true value of your business. If these potential buyers are not considered seriously, you may face a protracted marketing process that only attracts lower offers later.

Or it may be best not to sell, and instead continue operating the business until market conditions turn more favorable. Even if market conditions do not brighten, you will have gained the profit generated during the additional time you own your business. If you hold pat, however, you continue to run the inherent risk of operating a business in addition to gambling on maintaining or increasing its value when you reenter the market at a future date.

Unacceptable offers may indicate bad timing. As in most selling, timing plays a significant role in obtaining Maximum Value. Before going to market, consider the general economic trends. Then consider your industry and related industry trends to flesh out any potential buyers. Also, examine closely the most probable buyers and see if they are actively engaged in acquisitions.

4. **Provide solutions for the buyer.** With an objective eye, search for any negatives or problems in your business and be prepared to provide solutions for the buyer. Be sure to maintain balance in what you disclose to the buyer and when you disclose it. As a rule, be candid with the buyer. But if you present negatives, immediately have a ready supply of two or more solutions or positives.

   Do not let the buyer leverage those negatives to beat you down until the purchase price is driven into the ground. Remember the formula MP = MV and be ready to launch from all sides with your solutions, emphasizing a positive and profitable long-term strategy.

5. **Avoid post-closing liability.** The sale is completed. The champagne is popping. You've taken a big fat check to the bank (or it arrived there by wire transfer). Maximizing value means not giving back any portion of that check to the buyer.

   To insure that won't happen, make sure all of the transaction documents are properly prepared and completed. Attached to the primary purchase agreement will be disclosure schedules and/or numerous exhibits. These allow the seller the chance to make disclosures and "representations and warranties" relating to the business. The representations and warranties will address 25 to 35 different areas of the business.

   Post-closing liability usually stems from

improperly drafted representations and warranties and from the seller's failure to properly reveal items in the disclosure schedules. The manner in which each of the representations and warranties is made must be carefully addressed, as there are numerous legal and business issues to consider. The structure of the representations and warranties will then dictate the nature and extent of the disclosures required.

Even though the buyer may be fully aware of any misrepresentation(s) or item(s) not disclosed, you as the seller can still be liable for misrepresentations and failure to make proper disclosures. Buyer's due diligence does not relieve or reduce the seller's responsibility or liability. Please refer to the *Buying A Business* brochure at *www.MandAlawyer.com* for details on this most critical process.

Sellers should always negotiate for a "deductible" to offset future buyer claims. With a deductible, the buyer cannot make claims against the seller until the aggregate of those claims exceeds a specified deductible amount. When the claims do exceed that amount, the buyer should only be able to recover the amount in excess of the deductible. Sellers should be on high alert that buyers will almost always want to change the "deductible" concept and seek compensation for 100% of their losses if the buyer's claims exceed the deductible.

For example, if total claims are $300,000 and the deductible is $250,000, the seller will want a provision that allows the buyer to only recover $50,000. Of course the buyer will want a clause that seeks the entire $300,000, since the amount of the deductible was exceeded. (Buyers often use the term "basket" for this approach.) General rules of thumb govern the amount set as a deductible and whether or not the "deductible" or "basket" approach will prevail.

Establishing and maintaining a smooth working and mutually respectful relationship with the buyer is the best way to avoid post-closing liability. It is simply amazing how many difficult issues can be fairly and readily resolved if the parties have established a trusting relationship from the outset. And if the seller continues as an employee or consultant of the buyer, the ongoing opportunity to work together can ensure that minor issues do not become major hand grenades.

6. **Unity of sellers.** When the seller has numerous shareholders or owners, it is important that everyone locks arms.

Even though each owner's goals may vary to some degree, the buyer must not be allowed to manipulate that to his advantage while negotiating the purchase price. Owners should have one "point person" who communicates on their behalf. Each of the owners, however, has the right to participate in seller discussions with counsel, to receive full and complete information regarding the transaction, and seek their own legal counsel.

7. **Protect your business during the selling process.** Selling your business becomes a second career. For most sellers that means finding more time in their current 60-hour week. The sales process can become a major distraction from running and promoting your business. When this happens the business can suffer. That can directly impact your value during the 3- to 12-month selling period needed to complete the transaction. If the transaction unravels at the end, you may have sacrificed not only part of your current value, but also up to a year's growth of your business. As difficult and time-consuming as it will be, stay focused on what brought you to the dance floor.

DO NOT let your business slide by the wayside. The buyer needs the perception and the reality that your business is heading north, not south. This much-needed upward momentum will make it easier for the seller to prevail on many of the transaction issues right up to that joyous date of closing.

8. **Gain more value by staying on the train.** Often, a seller will retain an equity position in the buyer following the sale. This occurs frequently with "financial" buyers who need current management to continue to grow the business. That same management team may also be positioned prominently to attract other synergistic companies. Even though your retained equity interest may only be 10% to 30% of the sales value, that

ongoing interest could produce additional value that exceeds the initial sales price.

For example, a seller sells his business for $20 million and retains a 20% equity in the future growth of the buyer. If the new owner is on an aggressive acquisition and growth path that leads to a much larger company with increased value of $100 million, the seller will receive *another $20 million* at the time the buyer elects to sell. In some cases, the seller's retained interest may generate added value through an IPO by the buyer and registration of seller's interest.

EVALUATING NON-ECONOMIC FACTORS

Maximizing your value may mean more than just receiving the highest purchase price. A very significant human or emotional element exists in most transactions that should be addressed. Value may be determined, in part, by how well the seller fits into the company culture of the new owner. You must determine if working with the buyer will be a rewarding and satisfying experience, or one of constant stress and frustration. Ask yourself these questions up front in the negotiations to make sure you're making the correct decision. Frequently sellers want to protect their employees. This can be a highly charged issue. Therefore, the seller's desires in this area should be direct and clear early in the negotiations.

Both of these cultural and employee issues can be evaluated in economic terms. You may want to seek a higher selling price as compensation for a buyer work environment that you believe will be more strenuous. You may also want to deal for a higher purchase price and pass on the increase to loyal employees who you know are going to be terminated.

Finally, have you emotionally disconnected from not having day-to-day control of your enterprise? And are you ready to move on with the rest of your life? The answers to these questions affect sellers at staggered times and with varying impacts. Sometimes the seller experiences a great sense of relief and satisfaction. Other times, the entrepreneurial spirit lives on and the seller struggles with letting go.

Like many major decisions, your feelings will run the gamut from "Get me out of here as soon as possible!" to simply "Why am I selling?" It is so crucial to determine at the outset whether you are fully committed to selling your company.

But once you have made the decision to sell, seek the very best professional guidance you can find. You will learn that excellent advisors can walk you smoothly through the process. That guidance will help you get Maximum Value and successfully launch you.

Roger L. Neu, J.D., C.P.A.

Chapter 2

Before Signing the Letter of Intent

T HERE ARE SOME cash-saving caveats that should slow down sellers who are seeking instant gratification from their sale.

The potential to save considerably on taxes, increase after-sale income, and provide tax-smart vehicles for charities and heirs could *vanish* unless the following are thoroughly explored *before* signing the Letter of Intent to sell your company.

The heart of this strategy is to transfer a portion of your stock holdings to a newly created entity or charity. And, depending on the recipient, avoid paying Capital Gains altogether. Let's examine a couple of the most popular estate planning tools...

CHARITABLE REMAINDER TRUST (CRT)

The Charitable Remainder Trust is a multipurpose vehicle to avoid tax, provide consistent income for you and/or your heirs, and help a favorite charity, nonprofit or foundation at the same time. Here's how it works.

Let's say you transferred $1 million of future value stock

into a CRT before you sign that Letter of Intent to sell. After the sale, the CRT gets a nice bounce from the new company's public stock or cash. You sell the low-yielding corporate stock if you have to, or take the cash and invest it into fixed-income vehicles (see Chapter 8 "Fixed Income Vehicles" for investment ideas).

No tax has to be paid on the sale of your company and you, or whoever is established as income beneficiary, receive the income from the CRT. Although you can have broad flexibility when investing these funds, they cannot be used to buy personal items likes houses, racehorses or boats. The income beneficiary receives a specific income calculated off an actuarial table until their passing. Then the remaining principal flows directly to the charity of your choice, which could also be multiple charities or a family charitable foundation.

In a nutshell, you or your children get the income; the charity gets the principal. The insurance industry has offered an additional intriguing possibility called a Wealth Replacement Trust. It enables you to buy an insurance policy on the income beneficiary's life for the amount of the principal going to the charity. Finance the policy from part of the income and everybody wins.

CRT Advantages:

1. The money starts producing income on a pre-tax basis. If capital gains taxes normally take 25% away, your funds need to grow 33% to regain its former level; i.e., (100-25 = 75, or a 25% reduction; 75+25 = 100, a 33% increase). Your income would then be 33% higher than if you paid taxes and bought the same investment.

2. You receive the social/spiritual/global satisfaction of making a sizable charitable donation (takes care of years of tithing). While you must name a specific charity initially, the grantor of the CRT can change the beneficiary down the road.

3. These assets are now free and clear of creditor/judgment proof. They're no longer in your name: A future charity owns them.

CRT Disadvantages:

1. You don't own the money anymore. While you can invest and receive income, you cannot use the principal to buy a business, house or ranch. Although you cannot pledge it for a loan, you can borrow on your fixed-income stream. Sometimes this is a good thing, especially if you want to provide a steady income for someone but not give him or her the ability to spend it. (You know the kid I mean.) However, if you are a baby boomer in the middle of life, you certainly do not want all of your assets inextricably tied into a CRT. With 30-some-odd years to go, life can still have many surprises for you.

2. The wealth replacement insurance is expensive and cuts down your income. You will still be ahead of paying the tax and making the same investment, but you must weigh the net benefits vs. the limitations of future use of the principal.

Bottom Line: These instruments work wonders for tax-efficient gifts to charities or arranging a "hands off the principal" fixed-income stream. If you plan on giving a large donation to a charity, or dedicating a portion of the proceeds of your sale to a permanent fixed income-strategy, then you should definitely consider a CRT for part of your funds.

FAMILY LIMITED PARTNERSHIPS (FLP)

A Family Limited Partnership is a great vehicle to efficiently transfer "gift money" to your children, yet maintain control of the investments until a later date. Gifts of minority interests in a private company or property are worth less than their percentage valuation of book value or appraisal. Often a 30%–40% discount is used to establish a value at the time a gift is given. This is crucial as it can significantly increase the amount you can gift your heirs without gift or inheritance tax. The amount you can gift estate tax free is increasing to $1 million per person. This means you can gift up to $1 million tax free to you and your heirs ($2 million per couple). If you use a 40% discount for assets, you could conceivably gift $1,666,660 to your kids instead of $1 million without tax.

While an outright gift of pre-sale stock would work, redirecting it into an FLP first and then gifting that minority interest to your heirs achieves the largest discount. Plus, you can continue to gift $10,000 per year, per child ($20,000 per child, per couple) by continuing to transfer a portion of the partnership to your heirs. Your heirs receive the income benefits of their portion of the FLP.

If the gift transacts at a book value and the company is later sold for a higher valuation, you are able to transfer a larger portion of your wealth to your heirs, tax free, after the sale; if that is your wish. Once the transfer is made and the company is sold, the public stock or cash is funneled into the FLP. Income tax is then paid by the owners of the FLP (you may also be one of the owners) at everyone's individual tax bracket. This may further reduce the Capital Gains tax if your heirs are in a lower tax bracket.

Once the FLP has the proceeds from the sale, it can invest in virtually any item; e.g., islands, yachts, planes, etc. It can also unwind at a later date if you or your heirs want to invest separately.

Bottom Line: If you will receive more than you need for your lifestyle and security from the sale of your business, consider using an FLP to tax efficiently and transfer some off the top to your heirs.

These are two popular estate-planning tools of several you might want to thoroughly review. The captain of every new lump sum of wealth will have different needs. With the ever-changing estate laws, consulting with a top-notch estate-planning attorney before you sign your Letter of Intent to Sell is money *very well* spent.

Just like investment vehicles, you must balance your overall financial picture. An optimum estate plan with tax advantages and flexibility will usually come together from a combination of trusts, gifts, Family Limited Partnerships and "constructive avoidance"—or doing nothing. But in every sale situation, it is definitely worth investigating first.

Chapter 3

Evaluating Employment Agreements

As AN OWNER selling your company, you may be faced with the possibility of becoming either (a) an employee, or (b) a transitional consultant/ employee.

Many times you are required to do one or the other. If the deal is solely contingent upon your becoming a future employee, you'll want an employment agreement that is different than your status as an everyday employee in the new regime. Either way, like any new employee, you should know what you're getting into at your new position.

First and foremost, does your new employer really want you to even work there? I have a client who sold a large business and negotiated a one-year employment agreement. Since his previous daily duties were now handled by someone else, he was never told where he fit in the new arrangement. After a few weeks he had guilt feelings because he had nothing to do. He called me seeking advice. In turn, I called the lawyer who negotiated the deal. He simply laughed and said since the job was really part of the business sale compensation, he didn't even have to show up! But nobody told *him*.

Secondly, do you really want to work there? If you weren't

already an insider, would you truly want to work for this new combined entity in the position you're being offered? Or are you simply agreeing to the employment as a means to get your business sold? Ask and re-ask yourself these questions, as well as consult those you trust, before you start negotiating your employment agreement.

Keep asking "what if" questions. The more questions you can list, the better your contract will be; i.e., What if I want to leave? Can I sell my stock back to the company? At what price? Terms? Restrictions? If they give me a note and it defaults later, what is my recourse?

In my experience, sellers-who-turned-into-employees leave at or before their minimum contracted terms. The "downsizing" transition from running a small-to-medium size company to being an employee of a large company is too much to bear. Even when it's a good fit, the entrepreneurial spirit is so strong that it either inspires the next adventure or full retirement.

Bottom Line: Give yourself as much wiggle room as you can negotiate and still keep the deal intact.

Chapter 4

Creatively Managing
Concentrated Stock Holdings

M ANY PEOPLE ARRIVE at their new level of wealth with a large concentrated stock holding. While it is often derived from a business sale or public offering, it may also come from stock options, inheritance, gifts, bonuses, pension holdings or divorce settlements. Or often it is the accumulation of a heavily compounded business investment held over a number of successful years. But regardless of the origin of your new wealth, never assume your holdings will continue to grow at a similar pace or grow at all!

A recurring theme in this book is the value of diversification, and nowhere does its application become more essential than with a concentrated stock holding. Unfortunately, I have witnessed literally dozens of successful business owners labor for decades to build a business and finally sell it for Maximum Value, only to helplessly watch from the sidelines as their entire fortune tumbles when the new stock drops.

The usual combination of reasons for holding on include: a) avoiding paying taxes, b) unbridled optimism, c) no clear alternative plan. The very worst kinds of concentrated stock to hold are the shares of a company that are deliberately growing through acquisitions of entrepreneurial companies. Usually they pay the highest price and lose their key people within a few years after the acquisition. These key people were the centrifugal forces that made the target company prosper, and now they are less motivated as their hefty bank accounts have distilled their drive.

While owning a concentrated block of this kind of public company will make you feel like a king on the hill, do NOT, I repeat, do NOT hold onto it. In only one case I know of has the value of the stock risen. Every other time it just didn't go down, it literally plummeted 50%–90% within a few years, months or even weeks of their buying spree. In fact, one owner sold his company and received 1.1 million shares at $22 per share. It drifted up to $26 per share, missed an earnings report by 10% and then dropped like a boulder to $7 per share. The owner lost approximately $20 million in only two weeks!

My flat-out advice is to sell at least half right away. Sell the remaining stock if it drops more than 15% below your acquisition price or by the next calendar year, whichever occurs first. You do not want to jeopardize your entire future on this type of stock.

The best company stock to hold is a large-cap firm which is the leader in its field and pays a dividend that is at least half the interest rate on current CDs. The larger the company, the more flexibility you will have in selling, margining, writing options, hedging and exchanging funds. These are baseline tools for managing a concentrated block of stock. But by all means, do not have 50% of your net worth tied into one equity.

The classic sucker punch question is, "If you had cash in lieu of stock, how much stock would you then buy?" A sobering and honest answer to that question is the amount you should get to in a heartbeat.

FIVE OPTIONS TO CONSIDER

I. **Selling a Large Stock Holding**—Larger stock trades of 10,000 shares or more are considered "block trades" and require special handling by a block-trading desk. If a block trade goes to the floor of the exchange without a prearranged buyer, it will trigger a short price drop until sufficient buyers are attracted to the stock. This, in turn, will produce a lower sale when executed. The block desk can get a better price for you by using any of three techniques:

1. **"Working" the stock into the market over hours or days when larger buyers are present**—This blending allows the sale to take place without anyone knowing how large your position is. This is a particularly savvy strategy for thinly traded stocks or a "dedicated" sell program; i.e., systematically selling a certain amount every month to dollar cost average. Bill Gates sells millions of shares of Microsoft every year in this fashion.

2. **Finding a pre-arranged buyer**—Usually a large institution that already has a large position wants to strengthen their holding without running up the stock. This is highly specialized. Only a handful of big institutional brokers is able to locate the right buyers. (Many "wannabe" brokers try this.) Do not use your regular retail broker, bank or discount house for this type of

transaction. Commissions at this level are secondary to a smooth execution. Try the block
desks at Goldman Sachs, Merrill Lynch, Morgan
Stanley, Salomon Smith Barney, etc., or a third
market-specialist like Jeffries & Co.

3. **Using an "OTC Special"**—Large retail firms use
this technique to sell a significant insider position
to the public. On an over-the-counter stock, the
entire position is priced at about a half a point
below the bid. (This works even better if there is
a big spread between the bid and asking price.)
Retail brokers are alerted over the intercom
system that the firm has an OTC Special on a particular stock. Their clients can then buy the stock
between the bid and ask price. The brokers like it
because they earn a half to three-quarters of a
point commission (that's up to four times normal
commission). The stock is then sold to their
"easy" accounts. This works well for the seller if
no institutions are interested and the stock is
thinly traded. But buyers beware.

II. **Borrowing From Your Stock**—Borrowing on your holdings may be more attractive than selling for various reasons.
You can gain liquidity to diversify or buy real property, etc.,
without losing your "upside opportunity" or pay taxes.
However, it should not be viewed as a long-term solution or
a reduction of the risk of owning a concentrated stock position. Here are multiple ways to consider borrowing on your
stock:

Margin—If you have a listed stock or medium-to-large OTC stock, the easiest way to borrow from your stock is by using a brokerage firm's margin department.

The interest rate is relatively low (usually less than prime rate) and can be negotiated lower on borrowings exceeding $1 million. Depending on the current margin requirements, you can usually borrow about half of the value of your holdings. If your stock is thinly traded or under $10, the brokerage firm will lend you less.

The advantages of a margin account are numerous.

There is no application process—Just deposit your stock, sign the forms and you can have your money immediately. Secondly, the repayment is seductively easy. There are NO payment schedules. Interest builds up each month and is added to the balance of the loan.

If your stock moves up, they'll lend you more. However, if your stock drops below a prescribed level (currently about 35% of equity), you will get a "margin call." This will force you to lower the loan by depositing cash or selling stock within a few days.

Margin is a useful, short-term tool when used in modest percentage amounts. Yet only a few brokerage companies will loan on restricted stock. (Salomon Smith Barney and J. P. Morgan are two.)

Banks—Banks and trust companies also make loans secured by publicly traded (and sometimes privately held) stock. But the terms vary widely. If you have an ongoing relationship with a "private banking" division of a bank or trust company, start there first. If you're already known at that institution, often the terms will be better and the loan will be processed faster. If you have unrestricted stock of a medium-to-large company, most banks will accommodate you with loans up to 70%, interest only or termed out. If you hold restricted stock of a small company, you have limited choices that are mostly in New York and California. (Silicon Valley Bank and Softbank are active.)

Interest rates at banks are usually tied to LIBOR plus 1 to 3 points. Often, because the lenders cannot sell the restricted stock they are holding as collateral, they may request additional guarantees or whatever you intend to buy with the loan as collateral.

III. **Writing Options**—Option writing is an excellent way to pick up extra income and/or increase your sales price. In essence, you sell someone else the right to buy your stock at a particular share price, known as the "strike price," for a limited time period (expiration date). If you have a $40 stock, you might sell 3-month, $45 call options for $1.50. You receive $1.50 per share immediately to spend as you wish. In 3 months, if the stock is still *under* $45, you keep your shares and the options expire without worth. If the stock is *above* $45, you can either buy the options back or have your stock "called" at 45. Since you already received $1.50 for selling the options, your sales price is really $46.50, if called. If you are willing to sell your stock at $46.50, this is a good strategy. Yet, there are drawbacks. If the stock goes up well beyond $46.50, you must still be satisfied with your sale. More importantly, you have only given yourself $1.50 downside protection should the price drop and you decide to sell it lower. However, if you have a flexible time horizon, you could write options to sell at a premium price (called "out of the money") four times a year. You could collect significant premiums and lower your cost basis until it is finally called away. Many NASDAQ listed companies do not have listed options. In these cases, a private option transaction can be arranged for a limited number of shares. These are usually priced below market and have limited secondary liquidity.

Option writing is very specialized. It entails many more issues and risks than described above. Do not try this at the office by trying to write options yourself. I strongly recommend you request an "options specialist" at a major brokerage house as opposed to your regular broker, discount house or e-trader. Ask for a track record of a dedicated program. Do not ever go "naked"; i.e., writing options without owning the underlying stock as collateral, and do not speculate by buying puts and calls on securities. Leave that to the gambling crowd. I have never seen or heard of anyone making money in such a risky way over a multi-year period.

IV. **Stock Hedging**—Although writing stock options offers some downside protection, it is limited to the amount of premium ($) you receive for selling the call options. But there are several ways to protect your downside risk completely. This downside risk-avoidance comes at a price to you, or removal of any upside opportunity.

Options can be purchased instead of sold to give you the right to sell your stock at a given price for a specific time period ("put" options). Say your stock is again at $40. You could buy the right to sell your stock for $40, for the next 3 months, for about $3. If the stock drops, you "put" your stock at $40 by selling it to the put writer. But your real sales price would be $40 - $3 = $37. Fortunately, if the stock rises, you have unlimited upside potential.

It is also possible to execute a "cashless collar." This is when you buy a put option and sell a call option. The money you earn from selling the call option offsets, either fully or partially, the cost of the put option. Basically, this locks your price and freezes your position for the duration of the option period. A variation of this hedge is to short your own stock, also known as "against the box." Tax-wise, both of these "riskless" hedges may be viewed as a sale by the IRS.

If you have restricted stock—or even a large position as the result of a business sale—the company may place restrictions on your ability to hedge or short your stock.

Since shareholders do not look favorably on insiders shorting or hedging, double-check your ability to perform either maneuver. Hedging is also specialized. It's usually conducted with the same kind of broker who is experienced in options. Again, do not try this alone. Active management of your hedge position is worth the extra commission.

V. **Exchange Funds**—Exchange Funds diversify your concentrated stock holding, tax-free, into a basket of stocks that behave like the S&P 500. This reduces the specific risks of holding a single stock and allows you to spread your holdings without selling or margining.

Here's how it works: Along with a group of other people, you deposit your stock into a custodial account managed by a large brokerage firm. Depending on the size of the fund and asset mix of other exchanges, your stock contribution will be limited to a certain dollar amount. Once the Exchange Fund is fully funded, the manager buys industry and index options to allow the basket of stocks to perform just like the S&P 500, or some other index.

Exchange Funds normally have a 10-year life whereby you are supposed to keep your stock in place. During the decade, you are kept appraised of the funds' performance quarterly and receive a dividend based on the funds' overall dividend. After 10 years, the fund is divided and you receive your shares back, plus or minus the amount the Exchange Fund returned as a group of stocks.

Unfortunately, these funds are only offered a couple times a year and are quite restrictive. But, if your goal is to sell a portion of your concentrated holding and invest in the general stock market, this is an ideal method to do it with pre-tax dollars.

These techniques for managing a large stock holding can be implemented for a short-term event or as part of a long-term strategy. Keep in mind that none of them gives you the same flexibility as an outright sale. But each client's needs are unique, and often a combination of these specialized techniques can create an optimum balance of liquidity, diversification, and tax avoidance.

Part II

Building an Optimum
Investment Portfolio

THIS IS THE core section of the book; i.e., where the rubber meets the investment road. It will carefully guide you through to a worksheet that has a well-conceived asset allocation chart. The final document in this section will then accurately reflect *all* of your objectives.

First, I'll show you how to develop a healthy attitude for becoming a successful investor, including how to prioritize paying your debts. There will also be an executive overview on the potential returns and drawbacks of a broad range of investment vehicles.

These middle chapters describe in more depth fixed-income investments, stock market investments, real estate investments and investing in private businesses. By focusing on diversified investments you're comfortable with and an ideal team of advisors, together we can build a highly customized portfolio.

Finally, there will be a worksheet section to help you walk through the process of generating an investment charter, risk profile, economic assumptions, and finally, a well-conceived asset allocation that blends all of your investment objectives into an optimum (OPTIVEST) investment portfolio.

Chapter 5

Developing a Successful Investor Attitude

IF YOU'VE ARRIVED at your new level of wealth by building your business or by amassing real estate holdings—and are now selling out—your mindset may need to change. Very simply, the same set of skills, attitude and business acumen that helped you build your wealth might prevent you from enjoying it.

Although there may be a physiological and psychological letdown after winning the war (recently labeled "Sudden Wealth Syndrome"), the attitude adjustment occurs when you need to switch from being an active and in-charge manager of one concentrated asset (your business), to becoming a relaxed, passive investor of a diversified portfolio of assets where you relinquish day-to-day control.

While reaching the passive investor state is a worthwhile objective, it may take a front-end alignment to straighten yourself out and really enjoy it. The question you must answer is whether or not you really want to slow down. You don't have to. You could easily move into a full-time position of learning this business and managing your portfolio everyday.

Although you may become quite proficient, the odds are stacked against you for achieving better returns or less risk than by hiring competent advisors.

Sure, there are some happy and successful investors who have transformed a spare bedroom into a home office where they actively manage the portfolio, collect checks and daily monitor the various markets. On the other hand, I have also met many unhappy and dissatisfied investors because they didn't begin their new job of being an *investor* with the "right" approach.

That "investor" mindset will take a few years to master and will need to change over time as well. But your first step to fully enjoying "cashing out" is learning how to wear a new hat. This new "investor" hat is similar to changing your thinking and behavior as you make the transition from being a "bachelor" to being a "husband." You're the same person, but there is definitely a new set of rules and regulations you need to follow to maintain a comfortable status quo.

CONTROL

Perhaps your biggest unforeseen adjustment will come from a change in the commanding officer. Although you will need to turn over day-to-day control to your team of advisors, you can still create methods of monitoring their executions and tracking their performance. You can set down instructions and priorities and request updates; but sooner or later you will need to let them steer the ship.

If this is a foreign concept to you, take it slowly, one step at a time. Hand over more and more responsibility and gradually stretch out the time period between reports. Eventually, you will reach a comfort zone between running every aspect yourself and becoming completely passive.

In the first few months of freshly diversifying your assets and getting accustomed to new advisors, I would suggest weekly, not daily, contact. From then on, informal monthly updates and formal quarterly reports should be the norm. Sure, you can shuffle advisors and allocations. But if you've taken the steps outlined in this book and have done your homework, give your advisors reasonable leeway to evaluate their performance. I recommend a two to three-year time frame for stock and real estate investments.

However, if you cannot receive accurate or timely reports (within 60 days), or worse, catch your advisors in a lie or misrepresentation, then let them go. Unfortunately, every business, including ours, has its fair share of charlatans and dishonest people. If you're suspicious, give them an opportunity to provide an explanation. Misunderstandings do occur. But, regardless of the inside networking and political reasons for which you may be using these advisors, don't continue to work with someone you can't fully trust.

Keep in mind that trust, integrity, honesty, competency and acting as your objective and forthright advocate are the goals of all good advisors. Many are also wealthy, managing their own money as another large account. So pick advisors as you would a business partner. You will need their loyalty and, ideally, you may even come to enjoy each other's friendship. That can be a priceless bonus. I wish you well with your selection of advisors as they are the golden keys to your investment success and ultimate satisfaction.

RISK AND VOLATILITY

After control, your next-biggest adjustment is becoming comfortable with investment risk and volatility. I define risk as the potential for "internal" problems, like poor stock picks or incompetent management. These are tricky issues that can erode your investments regardless of how well the industry or economy is performing. Yet, you may have some influence over these items. I define *volatility* as "external" issues that influence what third parties are willing to pay (for your asset) at any given time. An international monetary crisis may have little to do with your local software investment business, but could decidedly affect the price of your stock. This kind of external volatility is difficult to anticipate and impossible to control.

After a while, you will learn the acceptable risks and levels of volatility of different investments, and will understand your tolerance quotient. My suggestions are to (a) assume normal risk/volatility, (b) have a definite plan for unacceptable risk/volatility (predetermined stop loss), and (c) diversify broadly to manage absolute loss.

While I could build an excellent portfolio with typical risk and volatility for you, it could take you a few years (if ever) to become comfortable. It's better to start with an extra-large cash allocation and normal allocations for familiar asset categories. Then, to diversify further, add additional categories as you learn their particular nuances. But remember, *every investment vehicle has risks*. Government bonds, CDs and even cash under your mattress have separate risks. You can't avoid it. Learn to understand and embrace it, minimize it, and then sleep like a baby on a mattress without lumps.

Your third-biggest mindset change should be in your communication expectations. Fortunately, if you are a large investor, you can preset how often and in what format you want to receive your information. One large investor wanted his complete portfolio faxed to him every night. For him we built complicated financial accounting models and tracked turnover rates, credit card charges, minutes logged, etc. Although this was an exceptional request, let your advisors know exactly how they should report to you. Ask what their normal communication procedures are. But don't be shy about designing your reports the way you prefer them, *if it really matters to you.*

As an OPTIVEST client, you receive a large notebook with custom dividers for your original investment allocation, current portfolio updates, meeting notes, project notes, accounting sections for various trusts, foundations, children's accounts, etc. Year-to-date tax information (also sent directly to your accountant quarterly) and a section to insert your brokerage statements are also included.

After a few quarters, this notebook is strengthened to include everything you need to keep it up-to-date, except confirmation of every stock trade. At the end of the year, we provide a bound and spine-dated, year-end volume that details that year's pertinent information. The prior year's information can be filed and the notebook starts fresh each year. You can adopt a similar system or scan everything into your computer.

If you can release day-to-day control to your advisors, become comfortable with the volatility and risks of your portfolio, and can create a comprehensively written electronic and verbal communications system, you're on the runway ready to take off and enjoy the total freedom that your investments should provide you.

Chapter 6

Simplify Your Finances

JUST LIKE MULTIPLE credit cards, checking accounts and club memberships, too many investment accounts are more of a hassle than a help. Your investments need to be diversified. Your custodial and reporting relationships do not. You only need one brokerage relationship, one accountant and one lead general-investment counselor who coordinates all of your portfolio's sub-managers on your behalf.

This lead advisor should act as a head coach for *your* football team. He devises the game plan and works with the players and specialty coaches. Yet *you* still own the team and are involved as much or as little as you choose. Your lead advisor should be in constant contact with your sub-managers—or specialty coaches—and should produce consolidated reports with a professional software package (we use Advent).

Unfortunately, you will always need several attorneys, but only one to advise you on your estate design. Be sure to choose one that is "proactive." It's much more beneficial to turn down half of his or her ideas than work with an attorney

who doesn't offer any. You only need one insurance professional, too. Select him for the large estate-planning strategies
and let his staff handle your lesser needs.

Once every quarter you, or at least your lead advisor, should
meet with your accountant and estate attorney together. Let
them interact as a winning team on your behalf.

Simplify your banking needs, too. Use only one large bank,
preferably one with private banking services which include
personal lines of credit. Become proficient with Quicken or
other electronic bill-paying systems, or hire a bill-paying
service. Remember, less daily management and less hassle
equal more freedom. But always, always *read* your monthly
income and expense report. YOU must stay on top of how
much you're spending and where it goes.

Chapter 7

Debt Reduction or Capital Investment?

O FTEN WHEN AN enormous pot of gold arrives in your account, a frequent first question is "Do I (a) pay off some or all of my debt (homes, business, cars, boats, etc.), or (b) invest at a high return?" The solution I always emphasize is balance. If you can write checks to pay off your debts, you should only carry debt for *strategic purposes*. Let me offer some suggestions:

Debts to Pay Off—

1. Any credit card or consumer debt

2. Any car, boat or plane debt not at a sub-prime interest rate

3. Any debt with a personal guarantee (besides your home)

4. Any above-institutional-rate loans like 2nd mortgages or lines of credit

Debts to Maintain—

1. Up to $1 million on your personal residence (it's one of your last tax shelters and one that may be difficult to replace if you've cashed out)

2. Business or real estate loans that are at or below current interest rates (these loans are not guaranteed and have positive leverage [cash flow after debt])

3. Leased equipment and/or cars that are currently fully deductible and easily supported by your business

The tough calls are debts at current rates vs. attractive current investments. If your cash flow is modest and unlikely to increase anytime soon, pay off your debt and don't risk the investment. If your current cash flow is a raging river, make your investments, and at the same time accelerate the principal reduction on your debt. If you have a 30-year loan, pay extra each month (while you are blessed with extra cash flow) to amortize the debt over 2–10 years. I like to memorialize the payoff time-frame to a personal milestone like a significant birth date or to coincide with a child starting (or finishing) college. If your cash flow ebbs, you can always go back to a 30-year amortization, but with a lower balance.

Bottom Line: Decide which debts you want to pay off *before* you begin your asset allocation. And remember, keep debt only for strategic purposes.

Chapter 8

Fixed-Income Vehicles

ISTORICALLY, BONDS AND high-yielding stocks have been the backbone of retirement portfolios for good reason: They provide a predictable cash flow and are readily liquid if you need the principal.

For individuals and trusts (as opposed to a tax-exempt entity like an IRA or CRT), this usually means municipal bonds, "munis," because of their tax-free status. Because bond price- swings can be as volatile as stocks, other fixed-income vehicles should be included in your portfolio to provide some inflation protection. Let's review your choices.

MUNICIPAL BONDS

Investment books traditionally define the safety of munis as second only to U.S. Treasury Bills. In a broad category defini-tion, that is correct. Defaults are around ½ of 1% per year and almost always come from non-rated or low-rated issues. However, lack of defaults doesn't mean your bond portfolio couldn't drop by 10% in any given year (like in 1994 or 1999). Remember, your income will be fixed, but your price will fluctuate with long-term interest rates. This can be managed in three ways:

1. **Buy long-term munis;** enjoy the higher return, keep your eyes shut to the price swings and hang on to maturity.

2. **Structure a "laddered" maturity schedule** by dividing your purchases in 2-year increments from 2 years to 30 years. When a bond matures, buy a new 30-year bond. (You will have less volatility with less income but you'll be able to keep your portfolio relatively current. Under this scenario, you actually want interest rates to go up.)

3. **Buy intermediate bonds at the "elbow" portion of the yield curve** (shortest maturity that gives you 85% of the yield of 30-year bonds) and plan on holding them to maturity.

While I recommend No. 3 to my clients, whichever choice you make, always buy AA or AAA bonds in your own state. Also, make sure they are tax-free and not AMT (Alternate Minimum Tax) bonds. These bonds will be the safest portion of your fixed-income portfolio, so don't reach for the slightly higher yields on lower-grade bonds.

Buy your bonds in blocks of $50,000–$250,000 from a major broker in your area. Make sure they hold at least $50 million of your state bonds inventory. This will assure you of a wider selection and currently priced bonds. Ask what mark-up is being charged since you won't find it on your confirmation. You should only pay ¼–½ point for intermediate to long term bonds and NO commission to sell them.

Avoid muni bond-funds. Even if these funds are purchased at a discount-to-asset value, the annual fees are too high.

Never buy on margin (you'd be surprised) and don't try to guess short term swings in interest rates. If interest rates are on the rise, and you can forgo some immediate income, dollar cost average over 6 months to 1 year.

As the safe anchor in your entire portfolio, municipal bonds should be 30%–60% of your fixed-income portfolio. Because of their stodginess and safety, you will generally find the integrity and trustworthiness of muni-bond brokers among the highest in the industry. Quality attracts quality: It's that linear.

CORPORATE BONDS

For lower income bracket accounts—IRAs, CRTs, 401ks, etc.—corporate bonds are more economical than muni bonds. While the same rules apply, there are only a handful of AAA companies. Even AA corporate bonds are rare. Most corporate bonds are BB-A rated.

With this disparity in quality, we use bond funds to create enough diversification to justify holding lesser-grade bonds. Our favorite fund, by far, is PIMCO's Total Return Fund. A product of the Pacific Investment Management Company, this bond fund has a yield that is somewhat less than alternatives (partially because they also hold treasury bonds). But the price stability and total return more than compensate for the lower yield.

We also like to use closed-end bond funds (fixed portfolios and maturities) trading on the New York Stock Exchange. You can often buy them 10%–15% below their asset value with excellent yields. But beware! They can be volatile with changing interest rates.

Low-grade bond funds, "junk bonds," can offer significantly higher yields. And in four out of five years, they will earn better total returns. Although these can be added to a fixed-income portfolio to "sweeten" the overall return, use them in moderation. Foreign income funds, like the huge First Australian Prime Fund, can yield even more but carry a currency risk. Used in isolation, these higher instruments are too volatile. Yet, as part of a balanced income portfolio blended with the following vehicles, they are a healthy addition.

SHORT-TERM INVESTMENTS

Treasury bills, agency paper, commercial paper and CDs are all cash substitutes. They should never be considered as real investments. If you choose to invest for six months or less, these vehicles, or a plain money-market fund, are useful.

With their federal taxability and high volatility, long-term treasuries are not usually placed in a wealthy-family account despite the ultimate safety of the principal in 30 years. As zero coupon bonds, they can be used effectively to fund your children's educational accounts or to speculate on swings in the interest rates.

TRUST DEEDS

Although trust deeds or mortgages on real property are simple on the surface, they can become very sticky if they fall into default. At OPTIVEST we have done tens of millions of dollars in first trust-deed investments without losing any principal. However, after taking properties back, fighting bankruptcies and managing different types of real estate, we have learned a few important lessons.

Yields on loans to traditional, institutional grade property are near prime rate. Most are underwritten based upon the debt-service coverage and can be fairly high loan-to-values. Unless you can borrow cheaply and lend it out for a nice spread on these types of mortgages, credit-based trust deeds are not great investment vehicles. Muni bonds or outright income-property ownership will return more for similar risks.

However, asset-based loans, sometimes called "hard money" lending, can be quite profitable and secure if you use the underwriting guidelines below. These loans are based mainly on the value of the property as collateral, not on its ability to service debt or the strength of the owner. The overriding criterion is whether or not you would profit (after expenses and hassles) by taking the property back for the cost of your original loan. Due to the high rate of interest charged on these loans, a real estate broker must negotiate the rate to avoid usury laws.

For general rules of thumb, here are some basic loan criteria (of course no substitute for a competent broker, due diligence and common sense):

1. **Only lend in a first position, first mortgages.** If you adhere to this rule, you will avoid 50% of the potential problems.

2. **Always get an appraisal.** Although paid by the borrower, the appraisal should be an MAI or reputable local appraiser.

3. **Always inspect the property and surrounding neighborhood.** Do some local price "comps" to make sure the appraisal is accurate.

4. **Use caution when lending on improved property or a finished pad.** Raw land in undesirable areas is difficult to sell even at $.25 on the dollar.

Feel confident that you could sell the property quickly for well more than your loan amount if you got it back.

5. **Get a Phase I Toxic Report.** Or get a Phase II report if the property has been used for industrial purposes.

6. **Keep your loan-to-value under 75% of recent cost or appraisal (whichever is lower) on income property.** Keep it under 60% on non-income improved property and under 50% on ready-to-build vacant lots. Real estate can go down in value and you will also need a cushion for expenses if necessary.

7. **Make sure the borrower has a clear exit strategy.** While you should do fine if you have to take the property back, your first choice is to be paid in full.

8. **Make sure you use an escrow and are properly listed on the title with title insurance.**

9. **If the loan defaults, don't soften after hearing a sob story from the borrower with promises of payoffs in a few weeks.** File the Notice of Default and start the 120-day clock toward repossession as soon as the cure period is past. (Every time I have relaxed, I have been sorry.)

If this reads like a lot of time and, likewise, effort to earn a high yield, you're absolutely right. It's also considerable work to select good stocks or real estate. But to build a trust deed portfolio, diversify your loans over 5–20 properties, ideally in a mix of types and borrowers. I usually structure maturities from 6 months to 5 years and often impound 6 months of interest and 1 year of taxes, then roll them into new loans as they mature. When underwritten properly, asset-based loans create above-average income with significant safety.

Where else can you invest in a vehicle whose underlying asset (the property) can decrease in value by 20% and you're still protected? We use a handful of real estate brokers who specialize in pre-packaging these investments. Please refer to our website (*www.optivestinc.com*) for highly regarded referrals.

VIATICALS

This investment vehicle is a product that buys the insurance benefits from a terminally ill person. It's not as grim as you may think. Actually, it's very humanitarian as many of these people cannot work to support themselves. While they are still alive, they are entitled to receive a discounted face- amount of the ultimate death benefit to pay bills, remain in their house and generally increase their quality of life.

About 65% of the Viaticals are patients suffering from AIDS. The "actuarials" in this business are surprisingly accurate and the policies are priced at 12% for 1 year, 13% for 2 years and 14% for 3 or more years. Like trust deeds, you build a portfolio of Viaticals with maturities rolling over every 6 months or so. You can also invest in a mutual-fund type of Viatical which yields about 11% currently, paid monthly.

Safety procedures are imbedded with escrows until the insurance company changes beneficiaries (and ownership), future policy premiums are impounded and health conditions are verified by independent third parties, etc. Pension accounts and IRAs are acceptable too. Your principal is guaranteed by a large insurance company as death benefits are regulated with 100% liquid reserve requirements. Life insurance companies are required by law to pay you the proceeds within 30 days of death. Death benefits are tax-free and there is no reporting. (Check with your accountant.)

Despite the simplicity of this vehicle and the safety of the large insurance companies, it is unregulated by the securities industry. This, unfortunately, has led to some Ponzi schemes and bucket-shop style marketing. Contact only the biggest underwriters which are presently located in South Florida. (We can give you referrals elsewhere as well.)

UTILITY INVESTMENTS

Public utility investments were popular retirement income vehicles in the 1950s and 1960s. In today's environment, they are not competitive instruments. Nevertheless, good utility companies increase their dividends every year and can provide a nice total return in a deflationary environment, or when the general stock market is in the doldrums.

Our focus is specifically keyed on private energy production facilities that have long-term contracts to produce electricity for large public utilities. These power plants—using natural gas, methane from trash dumps, trash, wood chips, coal and hydroelectric—can be purchased for about 6–8 times earnings (12%–16% yield).

Even without leverage, this produces significant income, and mostly tax-sheltered due to the rapid depreciation of the equipment. Sometimes the heat by-product of these energy plants can be used to produce steam, heating, refrigeration or even distillation, and offer a secondary source of income. Deregulation will make these plants more valuable with their ability to directly sell any excess capacity.

You can buy these plants outright and oversee the management of the facility yourself. But *you* get the call at 3 A.M. when turbine No. 3 goes down. At OPTIVEST, we've experienced better success by pooling our money with other investors and buying a diversified portfolio of plants (by type and geography) that are professionally managed.

Although your cash flow is lower, it's much safer and you won't have to deal with management headaches. We like Ridgewood Electric Power ($100,000 unit size) and Prudential's program ($5 million unit size). These have been some of the most popular income investments for our clients over the years.

REITs

Like a "good penny, bad penny," Real Estate Investment Trusts come in and out of favor on Wall Street every few years. They are organized like mutual funds except they hold income property instead of stocks. Unlike owning real estate directly, the public REITs are listed on the major exchanges and can be regularly bought and sold.

REITs usually specialize in a particular type of property like commercial, apartment, retail mall, office buildings or hotel. We prefer to build a portfolio of REIT stocks that are diversified over a broad range of types of property. The market price of these shares can be at a premium or discount to the value of the combined holdings.

When they are out of favor, it is possible to buy these REITs at discounted levels that produce income well above what could be obtained by purchasing a similar property outright.

Plus, the dividends grow as rent increases are made.

Like most investments, they should be purchased when they are undervalued and sold when they become overvalued. While it sounds logical, it's not popular because the masses will be buying high-flying stocks and seemingly making quick profits. If you're patient, in the long run you will make more money and sleep easier at night when you buy out-of-favor sectors.

INCOME REAL ESTATE

Although I later devote an entire chapter to real estate, I want to prep your future reading with the following.

Besides muni bonds, real estate should be a cornerstone of your fixed-income portfolio for several reasons:

> You earn relatively high income that's at least partially sheltered by depreciation.

> Unlike bonds, real estate will increase in value with inflation.

> As rent increases, your cash flow likewise increases.

> You can defer your capital gains with tax-free exchanges (Code Section 1031) and can refinance (borrow) from your principal without being taxed on it.

> It brings price stability, or equilibrium, to your bond portfolio's volatility.

If you can afford to purchase at least five properties outright, diversified along property types, do it. Otherwise, pool your money with other investors and purchase at least five small or large syndications with experienced managers. While the biggest drawback is lack of liquidity, that's why you have muni bonds, stocks and cash.

GETTING ALL YOUR FIXED-INCOME VEHICLES UNDER ONE ROOF

A combination of these income vehicles—with quality muni bonds and real estate comprising 50% to 100%—should produce a steady income and a positive total return (price change plus yield).

For clients pursuing a long-term income component in their portfolio, we use most or all of these various income investments (see sample portfolio). It usually takes 6–18 months to fully invest an income portfolio using these investments. Even so, you will be well rewarded with increasing annual income and well cushioned with stability and inflation protection.

Chapter 9

The Stock Market

Y OU'VE PROBABLY READ or seen many books with one stock guru after another claiming how to pick stocks, how to profit from the technical indicators, etc. Rest assured there will be an absence of technique in this section. Rather, I will present a macro-view of how best to use the stock market as an integral section of a well-balanced and diversified investment portfolio. Here are four successful investor profiles and some common mistakes to avoid.

1. THE PERMANENT INVESTOR

These are the Warren Buffets of the world. Buy big; hold forever. This works well for the few people who have actually executed this strategy. The best are "fine tuned" only every year or so. The trick here is to craft your own Dow Jones or S&P 500 portfolio with large industry leaders in every major category (worldwide). Tweak your holdings only when the leader falls from the top. A variation is to purchase three to five U.S. and global five-star mutual funds.

The advantages to emulating Warren Buffet's style are negligible sales commissions, low typical annual taxes and simplicity.

The disadvantages are that you are likely to get impatient and trade your account, or you choose a weak economic environment and abandon it due to poor initial performance.

This investment approach works best for long-term trusts, CRTs and UGMAs (Unified Gifts to Minors Accounts), etc., that need infrequent review and truly have a 10-year plus timeline.

2. THE INSTITUTIONAL INVESTOR

Most large ($50 million+) stock portfolios are managed "institutional style." You form a paid advisory committee of three to five stock-market experts from various industry backgrounds (i.e. bank trust department, stockbroker, stock manager, overall investment advisor, etc.).

Keeping *your* goals in mind, the committee develops an investment charter outlining the specific targeted returns, risks, volatility, beta, etc., of your ideal portfolio. Then an original asset-allocation pie chart is developed to meet the charter's objectives with a balance of stock management styles. This is usually a mix of big caps, medium caps, small caps, value investing and growth. Occasionally index, special situation management style or foreign stocks are included.

Once the allocation of styles is decided, you begin interviewing top stock managers for each allocation slot. Usually, the managers must have at least $50 million under management, five years consecutive experience in that specialty and perform in the "northwest quadrant" (less volatility, yet better performance than their benchmark index).

After implementation, the committee meets monthly to review each manager's performance and quarterly with each manager. In this situation, the stocks are held with a central custodian who does the master bookkeeping. As some styles perform better than others, the allocations are usually shifted back to the original asset allocation. This means you thin out the best performing groups and beef up the out-of-favor styles.

Although this kind of investing is time-intensive, it produces solid returns over a multi-year time frame. The essential key is to develop a proper investment charter and allow your managers a full market cycle to prove their mettle.

3. ACTIVE ASSET ALLOCATION INVESTORS

Somewhat similar to the above institutional style, this approach is more aggressive, as you are trying to predict the kind of management styles that will be the most profitable over the coming year. Often, only two to five styles are selected and most are deliberately avoided. Management styles usually go in cycles and will stay in favor three to five years.

Ideally, you try to buy into a style of management when it is first emerging after being out of fashion for several years. Hopefully, you'll sell when its valuations are at ultra-high levels. While it is possible to achieve superior returns with this technique, it requires close scrutiny and sometimes mathematical models to freeze your emotions out of making decisions.

4. THE "OPTIVEST SYSTEM" OF INVESTMENT

In light of the pluses and minuses of the first three styles, we design a customized stock allocation for each client at OPTIVEST.

For large accounts, we serve as the chair of the advisory committee and help create the investment charter. Then, we monitor the managers closely to insist they stick to their style and stated disciplines. If they are a value manager, we don't want them to own a "Cisco" growth stock no matter how attractive it is. We meet with the individual managers, and follow up with a report on our observations and recommendations to the committee on a quarterly basis.

For accounts with portfolios under $50 million, we first create an investment charter, and then select a group of managers designed to balance each other to offset volatility styles. Next, we meet with the managers and clients and review consolidated statements on a quarterly basis. Often we hire non-traditional managers to reduce associate risk (see Hedge Fund section).

On stock allocations within long-term tax-deferred vehicles such as IRAs, 401ks, annuities, or CRTs, we prefer a more passive approach. We build a global core portfolio of several top stock managers (sometimes index and international) and monitor them quarterly. But we allow an elasticity of several years to give the allocation time to perform.

HEDGE FUNDS

At OPTIVEST, we've had particularly good results with Hedge Funds. This specific style of stock management is widely misunderstood. It can be confusing because there are at least 27 kinds of hedge funds ranging from low volatility on a government bond portfolio to wild speculation in commodities and currencies.

There are two Hedge Fund management styles in which we've excelled:

Long-Term, Long-Bias Hedge Fund—Lousy name; great performer. It works like the permanent portfolio (buy big and hold for years) with short-term hedging techniques to minimize bearish markets. Sometimes this involves paired trades; i.e., long on a strong stock and short on a weak one in the same industry (for example, long "Dell" and short "Compaq").

Industry and index options are used on a formula basis to protect against general market declines. We use one such manager who has had an *average* annual net return in the high 20% without a single loss in 15 years. As a bonus, 90% of the gains have been unrealized, so there have been limited taxes.

Small Cap Opportunistic Hedged—Wordy, but wonderful. This type of management style can usually only be effective with less than $100 million. They are very active and trade small-to medium-size companies that often have low trading volume. Again, as a stop gap, industry and index options/contracts are used to limit downside risk. Some of these managers have made 50%–120% net returns in a given year.

On the down side, they might also go flat for a few years. If you can withstand extra volatility, these funds will have the highest multi-year returns. On a typical year, you will earn 25% long-term gains 50% short-term gains and 25% unrealized gains. These still work for taxable accounts (because the returns are so high), but are better in tax-deferred vehicles.

The most consistent results come from multi-manager Hedge funds, called Fund of funds. Consistent returns and greatly reduced volatility make these funds an excellent alternative to traditional stock management.

Most hedge funds are offered in a master limited partnership, or LLC, which performs like a private mutual fund. The funds and stocks are housed in an omnibus account at a major brokerage firm and traded as one portfolio. After the first 12 months, you can get your funds out quarterly. The main distinction with these funds is a juicy, profit-sharing performance incentive for the managers. Typically they receive 20% of the profits plus a nominal (1%) administration fee.

When researching performance, be sure you focus on net

returns, not just gross (pre-fee) returns. With this lucrative incentive, the very best stock selectors gravitate toward this style as they can potentially earn millions in fees in a good year. So look for at least a three-year performance with an R^2 or larger (twice the S&P 500 performance with the same volatility).

STOCK MARKET MYTHS, MISTAKES AND MAYHEM TO AVOID

In over 24 years of brokering, managing and supervising literally thousands of stock portfolios, I have seen many avoidable mistakes occur over and over again. Learn from these misguided approaches and avoid the following:

Stockbroker Managed Account—Brokers are paid for turnover, not performance. Senior management only scrutinizes a broker's commissions and problems, never the results. Sure, there are always exceptions, but they're not worth your time to find them. If they were really that good, they would be fee-based stock portfolio managers instead of brokers. Avoid altogether.

Self-Managed Account—Unless you made your millions this way, don't assume you can do it. It's fun and glamorous, but rarely profitable for long. If you must trade on your own, give yourself 10% of your funds, and the rest to the professionals. To do it correctly, you must follow an expert, develop a network of information sources, read countless charts and publications, and become extremely disciplined in your buy-and-sell criteria. You must have the fortitude to check the market constantly, including into the evening with after-market trading. And that's every day—no vacations or golf!

Even for my own personal account, I leave it to the professionals. Buy and sell managers, not stocks.

Options or Commodities—Never buy call or put options or write naked options. Don't trade commodities either. In my nine years at a major brokerage firm, I never knew of any account making money this way for more than one year. Besides, it usually ended ugly. Just say NO. With one exception: A long-term dedicated allocation to a well managed commodities fund is a good inflation hedge if you don't own real estate. Goldman Sachs usually recommends a 5% allocation, but consider this a portfolio hedge; definitely not an investment.

Prematurely Firing a Manager—If you've done your research and picked a top-performing stock manager with a five plus year record, give them at least two years to outperform their index bogey (sole target like in the movie *Top Gun*). Too often, I've seen managers disposed after only 6–12 months of weak performance, only to emerge as a superstar a few quarters later. Ideally, you should allow them a complete market cycle (up at least 20% and down at least 20%). All stock managers will go flat or under-perform once in a while. It may be the particular style is weak or their specialized management is out of favor. Expect 2 to 4 down quarters for every 10. If anything, good stock managers should be *added* to after a couple of down quarters.

Avoid Bank Trust Departments—at least not to manage your stock portfolio. These entities do not attract the top stock managers and usually only have one or two conservative (deep sleep) styles of management. If you want that kind of management, buy an index fund and save on fees.

Always Use an Expert For Advice—Since you don't have legal contracts written by your doctor, don't use your insurance agent to pick your stocks or stock managers. Insurance professionals have their place in a financial plan, but it's usually not the stock market. Nor should you lend an ear to your attorney, CPA or hairdresser (again, you'd be surprised) on how to manage your stocks. Seek and reap the advice of a reputable, seasoned veteran; there are enough of us available for everyone.

Chapter 10

Real Estate Investments

T HERE ARE ONLY two ways to make serious money over time. The first is ownership of a business (private and public stock) and the second is real estate. While both have a variety of types and risks, both investment categories should be dual cornerstones of any long-term growth strategy.

Let's explore the most common types of real estate investment vehicles and then examine specific kinds of transactions.

FORMS OF OWNERSHIP

Limited Partnerships or LLCs—For decades, this has been a vehicle of choice for smaller investors to acquire a partial interest in a real estate project. Unfortunately, the Limited Partnership format got a bad reputation during the 1980s when many of the "tax shelter"-based investments went bust. Since 1986, when most of the aggressive tax laws were eliminated, Limited Partnerships perked up and have done much better.

Keep in mind that the Limited Partnership (LP) or Limited Liability Company (LLC) is only a *type* of legal entity. What makes good or bad performers are the particular properties they invest in, the experience of the managing partners and the market environment during the investment holding.

This form of ownership is good because you can diversify among more projects. In addition, the offering memorandum (sometimes called PPMs—Private Placement Memorandums) is required to provide significant disclosures of the particulars of the project, management, market studies and most significantly, known potential risks. For better or worse, your personal involvement is completely passive. You will never get that nerve-rattling 4 A.M. call about a broken toilet. The management teams of these investments include some of the very best real estate experts in the business.

Yet these benefits come at a price. Your investment dollars will be diluted by front-end loads, legal fees and due diligence costs. Often only 80%–90% of the fund goes into the actual purchase price of the property. But, if you did your own detailed investigation and formed your own entity to purchase the same property, you would spend almost as much and have to do all the work (assuming you knew how to do it) by yourself.

The only real cost is the sales commission: a payment to your advisor for knowing your objectives and risk tolerances, doing extensive due diligence on the property, dealing with the fluctuating economic environment, working with managers, and closely reviewing dozens of inferior transactions they didn't show you. Like most investments, a good one is easily worth the commission. A bad one is a bad one, no matter how little commission you paid.

The best LPs and LLCs are small-to-medium local projects ($3–$50 million) with well-known local management. Look for a track record of completed and sold projects (round trip) and ask about their worst deal. You or your advisor should have conversations with previous investors. Ask if timetables and budgets were followed, how well and how quickly they communicated, about surprises, etc. I also ask for tax returns for previous projects. You must also check the manager's reputation, sometimes even hiring a private investigator (we have). The *bottom line* is, I would much rather have a great manager with an average project than vice-versa. Great pro formas are easy to find; dependable managers are not.

Tenants-in-Common—This form of ownership falls between owning a Limited Partnership interest and owning the building outright. Often, you invest side-by-side with Limited Partners (or LLCs) into a real estate project, but take a larger position (10%–50%). You will have lower acquisition costs (less front-end fees) yet still have the advantage of professional asset selection and management. In addition, you can diversify further than if you placed all your money in one building.

However, the main advantage of a Tenants-in-Common ownership is your future ability to enter a tax-free exchange (1031) when the property is sold. You must also agree to the future sales price, or you can block the sale.

The disadvantage of a Tenants-in-Common ownership is filling out all of the same escrow and loan documents as you would normally in a regular real estate purchase (and you must sign on the loan—typically non-recourse to you). If there's a lawsuit, you are also potentially liable for more than your investment. (In a *Limited* Partnership or *LLC,* you don't have this type of liability. That's the "limited" part.) Most Limited Partnership/LLC syndicators will let you acquire title this way if you put enough money up front. While this is the best way to hold a partial interest in a property, the application is a considerable hassle.

At OPTIVEST, we currently work with six different real estate managers/developers and have several more we are closely monitoring in the wings. If their program fits the kind of profile we're seeking, we will usually watch them for two years to see how they perform. Then we'll start with a small investment. If all goes well, we'll increase to a full 5% allocation (see 5% Rule). We're very loyal to those whose performances have excelled. When the economy hits the skids, we'd rather be with a knowledgeable veteran than a hot dealer with rookie experience.

Individual Property Ownership—If you can diversify with at least five buildings ($10 million or more of equity), you should buy real estate by yourself. If this is your field of expertise, you can probably uncover good investment property and manage it yourself.

Otherwise, you have two options: 1) Use some of the same managers who specialize in LP and LLC to buy and manage (at a reduced cost) individual properties for you, or 2) Work with a reputable institutional real estate broker who can also bring in a management team.

But don't get snowed into only one investment type. Spread your holdings over office, retail, industrial, commercial and multi-family properties. This will usually require different brokers and management companies.

Some investment advisors, like OPTIVEST, can arrange this for you. Although owning your own buildings is most efficient, you or a paid advisor must be an expert in this field, as there are a lot of risks and legal issues that will be encountered.

Whatever you do, do not buy single-family homes to rent out as investments. You will rarely break even with your monthly expenses. Even the ones that have a positive cash flow are lousy returns on your down payment. There are a few exceptions:

> 18–24 consecutive months in each decade produce outstanding jumps in residential real estate prices. With leverage, you can make money.

> Investing in new home construction which is very specialized.

> Buying distressed property at foreclosure sales or bank auctions. However, these are not passive investments: You will spend time and require expertise to emerge in the black.

Bottom Line: Buy high-quality investment property and diversify between 5 and 10 projects. If you can buy them outright, great. Otherwise, buy Tenant-in-Common or LP interests. We have made more money for our clients in this area than in stocks. But it demands more fortitude and due diligence as well.

TYPES OF INVESTMENT PROPERTY

Multi-Family—A classic inflation hedge, this is my favorite for retirees and safety conscious fixed-income investors. A well-managed apartment complex or mobile home park can stay in good shape for 30–50+ years and increase your income via rents every year. We invest with managers who examine 10–50 properties for every one they buy.

Their primary checklist includes solid physical structure, good tenants, improving neighborhood, limited direct competition and a positive local economic climate. A condo map (or the ability to get one) is a big plus and can often translate into a higher sales price than it could if presented as an apartment complex. In one blissful transaction, we made three times our money in four years by converting to condos.

Selling mobile home parks to tenants can also be very profitable. We prefer to buy seasoned properties (as opposed to new) where we can purchase them far below replacement costs in middle-class working neighborhoods: but no inner city, poverty projects or high-class properties. Just consider solid, clean, average apartment buildings or mobile home parks with 50–300 units. Expect 8%–10% immediate cash flow with 3%+ increases every year. Usually the cash flow is 50%–100% sheltered with depreciation.

Commercial, Industrial, Office and Retail—Leased by businesses, these properties are more susceptible to rent increases (and decreases) than apartments. Here we scour the map for locations with the best properties that have the best tenants. Yes, you will pay more. But you will have full occupancy and get the best price when you sell, whether it's a good market or a weak one. Make sure the properties are well-maintained; no one wants a half-rented strip center in a deteriorating neighborhood or an office building in a high-crime, high-drug section of town.

Especially with real estate, you make your money on the purchase. Look for a manager who really knows a specific area inside and out, not an out-of-town syndicator. Ideally, you should invest in a portfolio of multiple properties.

New Development—This is a very profitable and opportunistic way to invest in real estate for one to three years. Yet, it is seasonal, has up to 90% high leverage and is aggressive.

We have had considerable success with two types of new real estate developments:

> **Build-Lease-Sell**—In this type of approach, a developer locks up a piece of available property, designs a building, and secures a core group of tenants to lease the space. Your equity combined with a construction loan (we make the developer guarantee it) buys the property and constructs the building. Often the lender will require 25%–60% pre-leased before funding. Your capital-gain holding period starts when the shell is completed.
>
> Once the building is 85%–100% leased, the developer gets a "take-out" loan to pay off the construction loan. If everything goes smoothly, this take-out loan can return 25%–100%+ of your original equity (usually 12–18 months into the deal) with no tax on this return of capital.
>
> Once the property is seasoned for 6–18 months with at least one round of rent bumps, the property is sold for usually 12%–20% more than the construction cost. With leverage, this can be a 25%–50% IRR. Ideally, you roll your remaining equity into another project, tax-deferred, and it's deja vu all over again.
>
> But the real estate market is cyclical and you don't want to overstay your welcome. Use an experienced developer who has been through at least one down cycle successfully, and start investing in projects early in a recovering market. Avoid investing in a mature environment or during a downturn. Expect

to split the sales profit 50/50 with the developer, usually after a 10%–15% preference.

Build-to-Sell—Often the fastest projects, they have no cash flow to offset expenses if your timetable is extended. Here the developer builds or converts a building (or a tract of single-family homes) to eventually sell directly to a user. This can be a condo conversion or selling a building from one business to another.

Build-to-sell loans are more difficult to acquire and require more equity unless there is a known buyer in advance. Your advantage is receiving the "developer profit" in a shorter period of time, usually 6–18 months. A significant drawback is being taxed as a "dealer" at full ordinary income rates. However, if you can keep part of the project as your profit and lease it out for a period of years, you can convert it into investment property and avoid the ordinary income tax. These are the highest risk to reward projects and should only be 5%–20% of most investment pies.

So, by all means include real estate in your asset allocation. It adds a better balance to a stock portfolio than bonds as it can do quite well in inflationary periods (unlike stocks and bonds). Again, diversify and pick good managers, not just optimistic pro formas.

Investing in Private Business

PRIVATE BUSINESS INVESTMENTS can be very rewarding. But they do require "high maintenance" with long due diligence periods and ongoing attention.

Along with my clients, I have owned two car washes, a radio station, a chain of Jiffy Lubes, a chain of amusement parks, three assisted living centers, a chain of hotels, a barbeque company, a software company, multiple independent electric power plants and even a hockey rink. We've only lost money on one, broke even on two and have done quite well (200%–300% return) on the others. In addition, we invested into venture capital funds that target high-tech and Internet companies with outstanding success.

All these private business investments taught me a few things. Good people with appropriate specific experience make or break a business. Our disappointments came from inexperienced management who, for the most part, learned on-the-job with our money. It's far better to have a diluted deal with an industry leader than a fat deal with weak management (despite great pro formas, I've never seen a bad one when they want money).

You (or your advisor) need to stay involved weekly. Leave the day-to-day issues to management. But develop an overview format to review sales, receivables, payables, personnel, etc. Try to keep business details to a few important factors (e.g., cars per day, percent occupied, sales per employee), and chart the weekly progress. Let them know you want to hear the bad news first.

BUYING A PRIVATE COMPANY

Even if you've pinpointed a specific business you'd like to own, use a broker to show you multiple deals in the area of your interest. Every business has valuation models. The broker can help you evaluate similar opportunities.

Most companies, of course, are valued on a multiple of net cash flow. These are usually at substantially lower P/Es than the public markets. This is a hands-off type of business where the present ownership has little or no involvement in sales, or the quality of the product warrants a high multiple (five times earnings). However, with a dental practice or a small insurance firm where the owner is very involved, this hands-on type of business may warrant less than two times net.

Never assume what you think is "net" has the same meaning the broker or business owner defines as net. Sometimes it includes the general manager's salary and basic benefits. Make sure you're buying a self-sufficient company and not a new job.

Also, be careful when buying a "cash" business. We once looked at a car wash for sale. When we asked the owner to see the books (business accounting), he said, "You can count the cars, watch the cash register and talk to my manager. I'll show you my house, boat and plane, but there are no books!"

When we inspected a Jiffy Lube to purchase, we overheard

an employee ask the manager, "Should we write this one up, Harry?" Although we bought the business, Harry was soon written up with a pink slip and let go.

There are many, many similar stories. Mostly, you must assume your employees are going to steal and your managers are going to cheat unless you have safeguards. But since so many cash businesses don't have books, the good news is you can purchase them for less than you should because they have no written justification for higher prices. But please do your homework and check it out thoroughly!

Although potentially rewarding, small business ownership is very time consuming and risky. "Angel" investing (individual investors going into a start-up venue) must spread their bets and put their money into at least 5–10 deals. *Better yet, put that money with a good venture capital group. You'll get 75% of the profit (vs. 100%) with a higher chance of success and none of the irritating headaches.*

VENTURE CAPITAL FUNDS

A Venture Capital (VC) Fund is a huge crap shoot. It's like drilling for oil, taking a lark on an invention or backing an independent movie. You invest in 15–30 deals and expect to lose 100% of your money on 50% of the projects. Hopefully you'll score 3 to 10 times your money on a few and hit a couple of home runs with returns of 50 to 100 times. On average, VC funds have returned 45% annually since 1960 versus 17% on small public funds, according to Ibbotson Associates.

Most VC funds are offered only to institutions and large family accounts; i.e., $5 million minimum net worth to qualify as a "super accredited" investor. Harvard University had to trim its allocation to VC in 1999 because it couldn't buy enough VC funds to fill what was allotted and had too much money left over in the till. However, the money it did invest returned 57% over the previous 12 months.

As our chart shows, this is one of the riskiest, and potentially one of the most rewarding investment categories we participate in. In all but the most conservative accounts, we recommend *some* VC funds—even if it's just 1%—to capitalize in this potentially profitable segment.

When selecting a VC fund, look for experienced management above all other criteria. Ideally, the management team should have expertise in operating companies as well as contributors who are board members.

On the road to a successful IPO launch, there are usually a number of "rounds" of capital infusions into a start-up.

Development Stages of a Private Company

Stage	Level	Investor	Value
Initial	Idea in Garage	Owners	Zip
1st Round	Full Business Plan; People and Assets	"Angel" Investors	$500,000–$10 Million
2nd Round	Product Developed; Sales Begin	Early VCs	$3–$25 Million
3rd–5th Rounds	Hitting Sales Targets; Needs Growth Money	Traditional VCs	$10–$200 Million
Massage Round	Pre-IPO Funding; New CEO; Audit Books	Biggest VCs and Underwriters	$50–$500 Million
IPO	Fully Developed Public Company on Steep Growth Curve	Syndication of Banks and Brokerage Firms	$100 Million+

It is imperative to understand where your VC money is being distributed on the above chart. Obviously, the earlier the investment, the greater risk and reward.

The last rounds are the safest, but have less upside. I prefer the 1st to 3rd rounds. If this is your "risk" money, swing for a home run!

Chapter 12

Summary of Investment Vehicles

THE FOLLOWING CHART is a summary of the various investment vehicles discussed in the previous chapters. The investments are listed in descending order according to risk, starting with tax-free money market funds (MMF) and ending with Las Vegas. The returns on these vehicles will of course vary with specific investments and future changes to interest rates and other factors. I have included a "Probability of Yield in a Given Year" column to give you an idea of how much variance from its targeted return you might expect. The longer the time period held, the higher the likelihood is that you will achieve your projected returns.

An ideal investment has a high return, safety and liquidity. Unfortunately, no single investment measures up. But through a careful blending of these vehicles, your overall portfolio *can* enjoy those ideal characteristics. The chart that follows will be out of date almost immediately, but you can find an updated version on our web side at *optivestinc.com*.

Summary of Investment Vehicles

	Investment	Yield Return*
Cash Substitutes		
	Tax Free MMF	1–3%
	Taxable MMF	2–4%
	Short-Term Munis (Tax Free)	2–3%
	Short-Term Treasury	3–4%
	CD 6 Months	3–4%+
Traditional Core Investments		
	Utility	6–8%
	Muni Bonds (Tax-Free)	4–6%
	Corp. Bonds	6–12%
	Income Real Estate (Tax Sheltered)	8–10%
	First Trust-Deeds	10–12%
	Blue Chip Stocks	5–15%
	Multi-Manager Hedge Funds	10–15%
More Aggressive Investments		
	Viaticals	11%
	Foreign Stocks	12%
	Aggressive Stocks	15%
	Hedge Funds	20%
	Real Estate Development	20%+
	Venture Capital	30%+
	Small Business	50%
	Commodities	50%
	Las Vegas	100%

*as of 2/03

Probability of Yield In Given Year	Major Drawbacks
90%	Low yield, yield changes
90%	Low yield, yield changes
99%	Low yield, sell at discount before maturity
100%	Low yield
90%	Low yield, sell at discount before maturity
85%	Volatile, possibly illiquid
98%	Volatility before maturity
95%	Volatility before maturity
90%	Illiquid, 5–7 years
85%	Illiquid, 1–3 years
60%	Volatile, inconsistent growth
80%	12 month initial lock-up
85%	Illiquid, 1–3+ years
65%	Volatile, inconsistent growth
50%	Very volatile, inconsistent growth
50%	Volatile, limited liquidity
70%	Illiquid, 3–5 years
50%	Illiquid, hit or miss
30%	Hard work, big risk
30%	Speculators lose, use as hedge only
40%	House wins in long run

Chapter 13

Personal Objectives

(Know Thyself)

WHAT DO YOU want from your money? A bald-faced question, maybe the hardest one to answer, but it ultimately drives your asset allocation and investment decisions. *What do you really want* from your money?

Some want security, freedom or peace of mind. Some want a sense of accomplishment or fulfillment. Some people want to become immortal or impact humanity in some way. Some want to build an estate for three generations. Some just want to count it or just relax. Whatever your choice, do not skip gently over this question. Think it through and through, and brainstorm with your spouse, family and close confidants.

Try to pry at the core of what achieving your monetary objectives means to your life. Think of your money as a powerful tool to help you reach your dreams. Think Big.

What are your personal life goals, values and dreams? The tighter the focus on the purpose of your life, the easier it will be to map out how to have your money help steer you there. As Walt Disney once said so brilliantly, "If you know your values, your decisions are easy." Without this step, money is only a hollow measuring stick and not a well designed vehicle to better your life.

To help guide you to the higher road, write out below what end-purpose you want your money to do for you (us):

1. _____

_____

_____

_____

2. _____

_____

_____

_____

3. _____

_____

_____

_____

Once you have articulated your lifestyle goals, think of everybody else you'd like to help. Although every family situation is unique, the planning process is the same. In the spaces below, think of other people or causes you would like to support.

Family Members	Type of Benefits
Daughter—	Linda ($3000 per month income)
Parent—	John, Sr. (debt-free house)
_____	_____
_____	_____
_____	_____

Organizations/Causes	Type of Benefits
Local Hospital	Cancer Wing
_____	_____
_____	_____
_____	_____

Or maybe it's a dream house, or a new Gulf Stream that will require a special capital fund. Whatever it is, give it an allocation and design an investment plan to achieve it. Think long-term as trusts, in some states, can be established to go on *indefinitely*.

Build a legacy: Leave something that makes a statement and can benefit several generations throughout the 21st Century. Live large, dream larger and provide in perpetuity.

Often in major family estates, several separate investment plans are needed. This usually occurs when the needs of the immediate family are easily achieved and the family wants to set objectives for their children, grandchildren, educational trusts, foundations, etc. Each of these entities has their own specific value and income targets along with risk and tax concerns.

For example, I recently did an investment plan that provided a debt-free home, permanent incomes for adult children and money in reserve to create an equal future benefit for the young children of a second marriage.

Sometimes grandparents want to organize a dedicated account to fund the private school and college expenses of their multiple grandchildren. This has been broad enough to include cooking classes in Paris and dance lessons in a New York studio.

These types of "gifts" can be much more rewarding than simply including heirs in your will because they can benefit in the present (often when they need it most), and you can witness the benefits while you are alive. In addition, estate-planning designs can make these types of benefits occur without estate tax.

Now that you've clarified what you want your money to do for you, let's take a closer look at your personal objectives. Personal objectives fall into two categories: The first is your obvious financial goal or goals, and the second is the "emotional comfort" you will need regarding control, risk, volatility, communication and peace of mind.

Objectives are extremely important and need to be addressed to achieve a successful allocation. Let's examine each one.

FINANCIAL GOALS

How much *cash flow*, after tax, do you want from your funds right now? If you are not going to be working, this is very crucial.

First, understand how much you have been spending on

average each month. The easiest way to calculate this is to add up the total debits or checks written each month on your family checking account statement. Go back about six months to figure the average per month. Look for the single line item that totals your debits. Consider what current income you have and then how much is needed from your investments. Add a cushion for emergencies and travel. Ideally, 50%–100% of this total amount should come from a dedicated income allocation to fill this most practical objective.

If your employment covers your household living expenses, then cash flow from investments is moot. However, cash flow is often the by-product of more conservative investments and a visible way, for some, to measure their investment success. Eventually, you will retire and cash flow will become important. If you will need that cash flow in five years, establish some positions today in assets with increasing annual income; e.g., rental income from retail, commercial, industrial, or multi-family real estate.

Income is the first area I target for my clients. Depending on the resources available and lifestyle needs to support, it can drain anywhere from 10% to 100% of the portfolio. For a quick rule of thumb for how much capital to dedicate to income production, divide your annual income requirement by the current prime rate: $300,000 annual income divided by .08 (8% rate) = $3,750,000. This is the set amount you will need to appropriate for income production.

Now apply it to your needs:

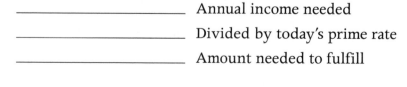

_____ Annual income needed

_____ Divided by today's prime rate

_____ Amount needed to fulfill

If you have funds to invest beyond your current income requirement, it is advisable to have a growth target and a purpose for the funds when it hits the mark.

Think about what you want the money for...future income? A mansion? Second (or tenth) vacation house? Educational trusts for children or grandchildren? Homes for your children? Debt retirement? Scholarship fund for your alma mater? Charities?

Pull your wish list together and write your ideas down with some concrete goals and time frames. Calculate what annual return is necessary to achieve them. Even if you rival Bill Gates in your wealth, you still need financial objectives to be responsible with your money.

GROWTH GOALS

Purpose	Amount	Target Date
1.		
2.		
3.		
4.		
5.		

COMFORT GOALS

How emotionally comfortable you are with your investment portfolio is equally as important as its actual performance.

If you can't sleep at night because you're worrying about it, it will never matter how productive your returns are. It's simply not a good fit.

This of course is very subjective, but I know I can be of some help. First, you need to completely understand your basic risk tolerances, which can be determined using the following questionnaire in Chapter 14.

Risk-Tolerance Questionnaire

BEFORE CONSIDERING ANY type of investment, it is mandatory to understand your tolerance for risk. It only requires answering five questions which will determine whether you are a conservative, moderate or aggressive investor. From these answers, we can begin crafting an appropriate mix of investment vehicles tailored to your ability to tolerate risk in your portfolio.

Simply circle the answer that most closely matches your investment philosophy:

1. **What is the amount of decline you can accept in a quarter?**
   A. None. *1 point*
   B. A little, but not for the entire year. *2 points*
   C. Consistency of results is more important than outside performance. *3 points*

   D. A few quarters of decline is a small price to pay to be invested when the stock market takes off. *4 points*

   E. Unimportant. *5 points*

2. **My investment is for the long term. The end result is more important than how I achieve it.**

   A. I totally disagree. *1 point*

   B. I can accept variability, but not capital losses. *2 points*

   C. I can accept reasonable amounts of price fluctuation in total return. *3 points*

   D. I can accept an occasional year of negative performance in the interest of building capital. *4 points*

   E. I totally agree. *5 points*

3. **How important is current income to you?**

   A. Essential and must be known. *1 point*

   B. Essential, but willing to accept uncertainty about the amount. *2 points*

   C. Important, but there are other factors to consider. *3 points*

   D. Modest current income is desirable. *4 points*

   E. Irrelevant. *5 points*

4. **How important is it to beat inflation?**

   A. Preservation of capital and income are more important. *1 point*

B. Willing to beat inflation, but other investment needs come first. *3 points*

C. Essential to ensure that you get a real return on your investment. *5 points*

5. **How important is it to beat the stock market over the economic cycle?**
    A. Irrelevant. *1 point*
    B. Prefer consistency over superior results. *3 points*
    C. Critical. *5 points*

Your Total Score From All Five Questions   Points

HOW TO INTERPRET YOUR TOTAL

Conservative—If you scored *less than 10 points*, you are a conservative investor with a low tolerance for risk. Your investment basket should include money market funds, corporate and municipal bonds, and all cash, income real estate and utilities that will preserve your principal while providing a steady stream of income. However, don't ignore the possibility of selecting stock managers who may be more conservative, as prudent investors will want to diversify appropriately.

Moderate—If you scored *between 10–19*, you are a moderate investor. You can accept some degree of risk in your portfolio for seeking potentially higher returns. A mix of bond and stock investments, income real estate, utility trusts and mortgages that emphasize steady income, along with the potential for some capital appreciation, would seemingly be ideal investments for you.

Aggressive—If you scored *over 20*, you are an aggressive investor who's comfortable with a higher degree of risk in pursuit of substantial rewards. As long as you are at ease "riding out" short-term fluctuations in the marketplace, you should consider an investment portfolio of U.S. and foreign stock investments, development real estate projects, hedge funds and new business ventures that strive for long-term growth. Also consider diversifying your portfolio with an appropriate allocation of assets in aggressive corporate bonds.

Your Risk Philosophy vs. Your Return Expectations

	Return Target	% Probability of Return in 1 Year	% Probability of Return in 5 Years
Conservative	5–8%	90%	95%
Moderate	8–13%	80%	90%
Aggressive	14–29%	70%	80%

RISK OVER TIME

Successful investing is frequently defined as the intersection of risk and time. Seasoned investors are well aware that time can help diminish the impact of risk since, over time, the effects of short-term volatility may be less consequential than the potential for higher returns when investing for the long term.

There is often a risk-to-reward trade-off; i.e., investors must be willing to assume additional risks when making investments (such as aggressive growth investments) to harvest higher returns. Keep in mind that if you allow risk avoidance to dominate your investment strategy, you become a servant to the earnings on your investment (when reduced by inflation) that could provide scant opportunity for you to ever achieve your investment objectives. In short, there is no such animal as a "risk-free" investment strategy.

Once you've come to grips with your risk tolerance and can closely classify your investment philosophy, you can focus on other intangible investment issues.

CONTROL

If you're coming from the business world where you owned and ran a company, giving up control is probably quite unsettling.

You have two choices. The first is that you can continue to maintain control by developing a home office empire and hub management style where all your advisors report to you. You *will* maintain control, but at the expense of creating a new full-time job for yourself in an area where you are at best an experienced amateur with, most importantly, your total net worth at stake. However, surrounded by experts whose advice you trust and actually use, you can make this work. This is how at least half of the business sale "retirees" manage their portfolios (see "Setting up a Home Office").

Or, you can gradually release control of implementing and monitoring the asset allocations, but not the *decision-making* of those allocations.

Often, it is most advantageous to have a good generalist as a "lead advisor." He, in turn, is a roundhouse of information, coordinating constantly with sub-advisors like real estate managers, stock and bond managers, private business owners, venture capitalists, etc.

LIQUIDITY

This is like a teeter-totter, balancing "what's practical" with "what's comfortable" in your particular asset allocation. While you may be aggressive for direct investments into real estate or business, you are also passive and tempered by your need for liquidity.

You can resolve this inner conflict by asking yourself, "How much liquidity do I *practically* need? How much do I need emotionally?" If you have a large portfolio, the old rule of thumb of having six months of living expenses is inadequate.

Try to predict what expenditures you'll be making over the next couple of years. Any big purchases on the horizon? Perhaps you want to pay off your debts (mortgages, cars, planes, boats)?

Outside of known liquidity needs, a conservative investor usually has 60%–100% liquidity (stocks, bonds, etc., for ready sale); a moderate investor has 40%–70% liquidity; and an aggressive investor has 0%–50% liquidity.

PERSONAL INVESTMENT CHARTER

Once you know what you want from your money and have defined your personal objectives; assessed your risk tolerance; set your income expectations, growth targets and timetables; and arranged your control and communication procedures with your lead advisor, you are ready to create a personal investment charter or mission statement.

This doesn't need to be eloquent, just accurate. Here's an example:

VAN MOURICK FAMILY
INVESTMENT PORTFOLIO CHARTER

Risk Tolerance	Aggressive
Value Goals	Security and freedom to spend time with family; offer pro bono financial counseling and continue activities with Christian ministries.
Income Target	$400,000 annually; as tax sheltered as possible
Growth Target	$10,000,000 for children and charities
Timetables	4 years for income; 6 years for growth
Targeted Return	12% after tax, calculated from what I have now to where I want to go, given my timetable
Volatility Goal	No down years; 5% variation from target
Liquidity Need	25%
Communication	Monthly on everything
Expectation	Self: Sub-advisors handle specific
Control	parts of portfolio

Now it's your turn! Start with the answers from the previous section:

Value Goals   _____

_____

_____

Risk Tolerance   _____

_____

Income Target   _____

_____

_____

Growth Target   _____

_____

_____

Timetables   _____

_____

_____

Targeted Return—You will need a "time value of money" (TVM) calculation to compute this. Accountants, real estate agents and college students have them.

Volatility Goal   _____

Liquidity Need   _____

Communication   _____

Expectation   _____

Control   _____

Chapter 15

Asset Allocation
and Risk Pyramids

INVESTMENT STUDIES SHOW that 80%–
90% of your portfolio's overall performance is tied to your
asset allocation, not your individual stock, bond or real estate
selection. During a stock market crash, your management
style and selections will have less importance than whether or
not you had investments in the stock market at all.

High-performance asset allocation is a pure art, not a science dictated by a computer program or by a formula for a
classification of investment aggressiveness. This art is dynamic
and matches the investor's present risk, return, volatility,
taxes, liquidity and comfort objectives with the present and
predicted financial market trends.

But it must be flexible because your objective *may* change
and the financial market *will* definitely change.

No two serious investors are alike. However, based on hundreds of initial personalized portfolio designs for a variety of
wealthy clients, I'd like to offer some recommendations on
both personal objectives and economic trends.

Imagine yourself sitting in my office. Now let me walk you

through how I could help you. Give yourself ample time to read and thoughtfully fill in the blanks below. Even if you have a financial plan, confirm it is current by going through the process again.

RISK PYRAMID

For Moderate Investor

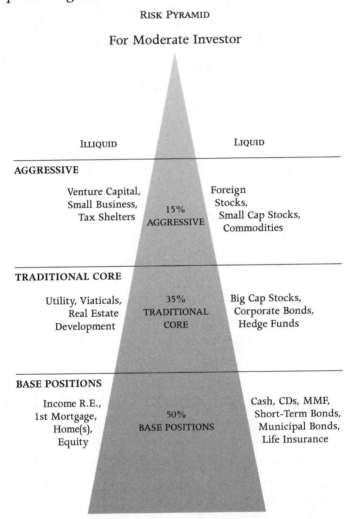

ILLIQUID		LIQUID

AGGRESSIVE

Venture Capital, Small Business, Tax Shelters — 15% AGGRESSIVE — Foreign Stocks, Small Cap Stocks, Commodities

TRADITIONAL CORE

Utility, Viaticals, Real Estate Development — 35% TRADITIONAL CORE — Big Cap Stocks, Corporate Bonds, Hedge Funds

BASE POSITIONS

Income R.E., 1st Mortgage, Home(s), Equity — 50% BASE POSITIONS — Cash, CDs, MMF, Short-Term Bonds, Municipal Bonds, Life Insurance

As a Moderate Investor, you should put more money in safer investments than in aggressive investments. You must also balance liquid with illiquid as well.

RISK PYRAMID

For Aggressive Investor

40%
AGGRESSIVE

60%
TRADITIONAL CORE

Little or No
BASE POSITIONS

RISK PYRAMID

For Conservative Investor

0%
AGGRESSIVE

30%
TRADITIONAL CORE

70%
BASE POSITIONS

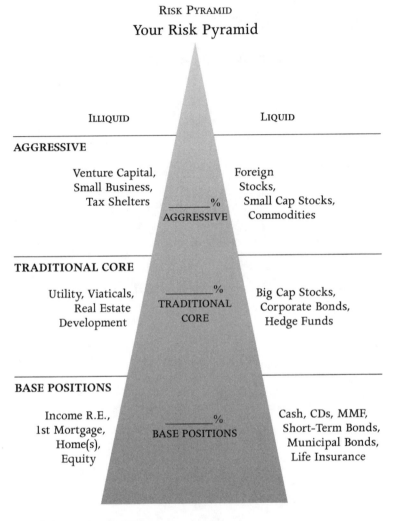

RISK PYRAMID
Your Risk Pyramid

ILLIQUID   LIQUID

AGGRESSIVE

Venture Capital,   Foreign
Small Business,   Stocks,
Tax Shelters   _____%   Small Cap Stocks,
                AGGRESSIVE   Commodities

TRADITIONAL CORE

Utility, Viaticals,   _____%   Big Cap Stocks,
Real Estate   TRADITIONAL   Corporate Bonds,
Development   CORE   Hedge Funds

BASE POSITIONS

Income R.E.,   Cash, CDs, MMF,
1st Mortgage,   _____%   Short-Term Bonds,
Home(s),   BASE POSITIONS   Municipal Bonds,
Equity   Life Insurance

Total Net Worth: $_____

Just fill in your *first instincts* on percentages among Aggressive, Traditional Core and Base Positions. Refer back to your Risk Profile. Then simply circle the investment vehicles you want to use. to refresh, check various chapters to get up to speed on each one.

Chapter 16

Broadstroking Economic Trends

ONCE YOU'VE CONSTRUCTED your Asset Allocation Pyramid, you must still evaluate the current economic climate before you mesh it all together into a logical investment allocation.

Where are we today in the U.S. business cycle compared to historical norms? Are real estate prices peaking? Or coming out of the doldrums? Are we overdue for a pause? How about interest rates and the stock market?

All markets have up and down cycles. So, we must first recognize where we are in each cycle, then decide if you should be aggressive or defensive in each asset category.

Here are my broadstroke ground rules:

1. **Invest most of your money in markets that have definitely started recovering from undervaluation,** and hold pat until they level off in overvaluation territory. You won't hit the peak or bottom, but you should enjoy most of the ride.

2. **In late stage markets or downturns, it's better to be a lender than an owner.** But don't buy junk. Invest in high-grade bonds for financial markets and high-quality first trust deeds for a real estate substitute. You may not be able—or it may not be wise—to sell your illiquid investments prematurely. If they're quality, you'll ride out the valleys okay; just don't follow it with new money until another upturn is obvious.

3. **Don't try to predict the bottom.** This has been compared to catching a falling knife.

4. **Don't try to predict the top.** I think I have picked "eight of the last two tops" (been fooled six times).

5. **Remember: Investment real estate and business (stocks) are the only long-term growth categories.** Build and keep core positions in both. Go for development real estate and aggressive stocks only in solid bull markets. And never, ever, be the last one to leave the party.

6. **Bonds can be as volatile as stocks.** Buy quality, quality, quality, quality. Limit your maturities to 8–12 years and close your eyes to the price swings. So far, a new multi-year trend occurs every time the prime changes three times in the same up or down direction. If rates are rising, shorten your maturities. If they're falling, lengthen your maturities.

7. **Don't invest in markets that are near historically high valuations.** Stocks at 30 P/Es and cap rates of 6 are not something to hold for the long term. Keep your powder dry. These markets may go higher, but eventually they all return to their norms.

We have a saying that "Spikes turn into cones." Let me illustrate what I mean:

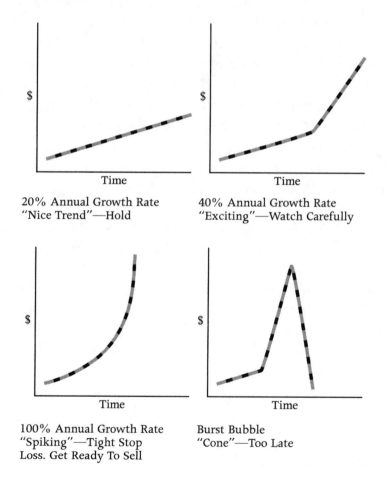

20% Annual Growth Rate
"Nice Trend"—Hold

40% Annual Growth Rate
"Exciting"—Watch Carefully

100% Annual Growth Rate
"Spiking"—Tight Stop
Loss. Get Ready To Sell

Burst Bubble
"Cone"—Too Late

INFLATION—THE KEY TO
ALL INVESTMENT TRENDS

Understanding how inflation affects investments and correctly forecasting inflation's direction are the most important factors in determining the future trend of every investment marketplace: stocks, bond, real estate...every marketplace. If you understand inflation, you will have the wind at your back.

Inflation has averaged 3–4% over the last 200 years. The first level of understanding is whether today's rate of inflation is above or below this average. The most popular index is the government CPI or Consumer Price Index. The U.S. CPI peaked in 1980 at 14.8% and fell to 1.2% in 2002. Inflation levels below 0% are called deflation, the kind of debilitating economic climate that Japan has suffered with since 1990, and the cause of the Great Depression of the 1930s.

If you overlay a multi-year chart of inflation with the prices of stocks, bonds or real estate, you will see an amazing correlation. Let's take each market separately:

Bonds—This is the easiest market to visualize because interest rates are high (and prices low) when inflation is high. Back when inflation was at 14.8%, money market funds were yielding 20% and long-term bonds were 12–15%. Of course when inflation dropped, interest rates came down and bond prices went up. Clearly, a falling inflation environment favors bond returns because you receive a high relative yield and your principal appreciates.

Conversely, when inflation is rising, your existing bonds have a lower relative yield (compared to new higher yielding bonds) and your principal goes down. Yes, most bonds will come back to par (100%) at maturity. However, I have seen

AAA rated bonds go down as much as 70% of their face value before coming back to even. Obviously, you want to own long-term bonds only when inflation is falling, and shorten maturities, or avoid bonds altogether when inflation is rising.

One way to gage the direction of inflation is to see how the pros are betting. If expectations are for steady inflation, the yield curve chart, showing government interest rates from 30 days to 30 years, will rise only modestly (maybe 2%). If expectations are for rising inflation, the yield curve will be steep, with long-term rates much higher than short-term (3–5%). If the yield curve is inverted, with short-term rates higher than long-term rates, then there is a general expectation that inflation is falling.

Pay attention or hire someone that will. The direction of inflation will directly determine the performance of bonds, and you need to modify your holdings accordingly.

Stocks—Most people, even professional investors, are not aware that stocks have just as much correlation with inflation as bonds do. P/E ratios, the main indicator of stock valuations, move in lockstep with inflation, but inversely. When inflation is high, P/E levels are low (and vice versa). Pick an inflation rate and I can show you where P/E ratios will be. Since 1920, inflation has averaged 4% and P/E ratios 14. When inflation peaked in the early 1980s, P/E ratios bottomed at 7. When inflation bottomed in 2002, P/E ratios topped out at 30 (S&P 500).

Clearly, when inflation is falling, P/E ratios climb. This "multiple expansion" turbo charges stock prices as investors pay higher prices. It's during these times that the stock market has higher than normal (8–9%) returns. If inflation remains constant, then P/E ratios remain constant, and stock prices simply rise as fast as earnings growth (4–6%). However, when inflation rises, P/E ratios go down—lowering stock prices even with normal earning growth.

Every long-term bull market has been accompanied by falling inflation. Most long-term bear markets have had rising inflation. The last bull market started after inflation peaked (1983) and ended when inflation started to bottom (2000). The last bear market started when inflation bottomed (1966) and ended when inflation peaked. The exception is the Great Depression when the bear market was accompanied by deflation (like Japan's bear market of 1990–2003). These are very significant trends. If you are in a rising inflation environment (or if inflation can't go any lower), stay out of the general stock market. Use multi-manager hedge funds, dynamic asset allocation or trend following market timing. The direction of inflation controls the long-term stock market trend. Don't bet against it.

Real Estate—Yes, by now you have guessed that real estate does better in rising or high inflation environments. Home prices will also rise, but they do not make good long-term economic investments, other than for personal use. Apartments, industrial, office and retail buildings do better because rents far exceed operating and financing costs, and you can pass along annual increases easier.

During periods of low inflation, investors expect the majority of their total return to come from rental income vs. appreciation. Buildings are priced relatively low, to return enough cash flow to make this enticing. If inflation is high, buildings are priced relatively high, because expectations are for appreciation (not income) to compose the majority of investor total return. If inflation is running at 8% and your money is leveraged 3:1 (75% mortgage), you expect to have large capital gains and income is less important. Conversely, if inflation is at 2%, you will want high cash flow to give you a decent return.

The best time to buy real estate is when inflation is very low (near 0%) and likely to rise in the years ahead. You will lock in an above average cash flow (8–10%) and be set to enjoy exceptional appreciation when inflation rises and prices escalate. Inflation peaks are harder to predict because, how high is high? Nevertheless, once the long-term trend has changed from rising inflation to falling, after years of going up, it's time to lighten up on your real estate holdings and invest more in stocks and bonds.

Business cycles, regional economies, national and world events will all influence the short-term direction of investment markets. Use them to enter or exit markets, always staying on the right side of the major trend—inflation.

LIST YOUR ASSUMPTIONS OF TODAY'S ECONOMY AND MARKETS

Please don't refer to the next section until you have an assumption on each of the following areas. If you don't know—or want to double-check—ask the most experienced expert you know in each field.

Even those experts won't be 100% right on this list, but you need to make an *assumption* before you make your allocations. Diversification will bail you out if your assumptions are askew.

Cycle Stage

Category	Early (Low)	Middle	Late (High)	Don't Know
General Economy	_____	_____	_____	_____
Stock Market	_____	_____	_____	_____
Long-Term Interest Rates	_____	_____	_____	_____
Local Real Estate	_____	_____	_____	_____
Inflation	_____	_____	_____	_____

Chapter 17

Putting It All Together
A Sample Asset Allocation

H ERE'S A SAMPLE portfolio with a 12% target return and moderate risk profile (without home equity and life insurance). It's flexible too. Change a decimal point and this portfolio could work for $5 million to $500 million.

(See next page for chart.)

A Sample Asset Allocation

Asset	Amount $	Yield %	Amount $	Growth[4] %
Tax Free MMF	1,000,000	3.0	30,000[5]	0
S.T. Muni Bonds	4,000,000	3.5	140,000[5]	0
Utilities	3,000,000	7.0	210,000	2
L.T. Munis	5,000,000	5.5	275,000	0
Income R.E.	10,000,000	9.0	900,000	3
Viaticals	2,000,000	11.0	220,000	0
Blue Chip Stks.	10,000,000	1.0	100,000	9[1]
Hedged Stks.	5,000,000	0.0	0	20[1]
Foreign Stks.	3,000,000	0.0	0	15[1]
R.E. Devel.	5,000,000	0.0	0	20
Venture Capital	2,000,000	0.0	0	30
TOTALS	$50,000,000	3.7%	$1,875,000	8.6%

Amount $	Total %	Amount $	Volatility[2] %	Portfolio %
0	3.0	30,000	0	2
0	3.5	140,000	1	8
60,000	9.0	270,000[3]	2	6
0	5.5	275,000	3	10
300,000	12.0	1,200,000[3]	4	20
0	11.0	220,000	3	4
900,000	10.0	1,000,000	6	20
1,000,000	20.0	1,000,000	10	10
450,000	15.0	450,000	8	6
1,000,000	20.0	1,000,000[3]	10	10
600,000	30.0	600,000[3]	30	4
$4,310,000	12.3%	$6,185,000	6.3%	100%

Chart notes:
1. Estimated return from stock managers during next five years (historical returns are higher)
2. Typical volatility, not maximum
3. Tax advantaged return—depreciation and long-term capital gains
4. Estimated 5-year average annual growth
5. Tax-free, after tax or tax credit.

This asset allocation has a return target of about 12% which would be appropriate for a moderate investor (typical of many of OPTIVEST's clients).

More importantly, it is achieved with significant tax advantage. Assuming maximum state and federal gains, personal income taxes and the use of 1031 exchanges on the real estate only, about $1 million of tax would be due (or accrued on unrealized gains). This reduces the annual portfolio return to about 10.37% after tax, which is *equivalent to a 20%* pre-tax return on ordinary income. Equally important, it is well balanced and diversified, yet has 56% liquidity ($28 million) within three days.

Each of these investments is discussed in other chapters of the book. However, I want to emphasize that there should be a rolling coordination of these investments.

For example, if more income is desired, additions should be made to muni bonds, utilities and income real estate. (Notice how these inflationary and deflationary investments are paired.) Prime funds—which yield about the same as prime rate or trust deeds—can also be used effectively for a low volatility income substitute. But they are not tax advantaged.

If more growth is desired, increase your allocations in stocks, venture capital and real estate development. Additions for growth can include long-term timber and commodities in small lots. Be aware of the volatility estimates, though. Growth assets *are not* an annual steady producer like income assets. Volatility is real and needs to be anticipated. Fortunately, it can be balanced.

Financial assets (stocks and bonds) usually move in an opposite direction from hard assets (real estate, commodities, collectibles). Note that bonds *are not* a potent hedge against the volatility of stocks. Some assets, like Viaticals, trust deeds and small business investments are not tied to the general economy and may go up or down regardless of economic trends.

This is the beauty of diversification. You have much better odds of reaching your goals in any given year and it reduces your overall risk. A portfolio of just stocks and bonds, or just real estate, will be more volatile (and less predictable) than most passive investors are willing to accept.

Furthermore, no single investment within an asset category should ever be more than 5% of your overall portfolio; i.e., *single* stock, real estate project, bond, etc. This requires you to further diversify *within* your asset allocation.

Now let's devise *your* asset allocation.

YOUR Asset Allocation

Now we come to the moment of truth. This is where you put your values, financial goals, comfort goals and predicted economic trends into an optimum Asset Allocation. Don't worry about specific investments yet. Just balance the investment categories with your objectives.

Using the "Investment Vehicles" section of this book (that are updated frequently on our website at *www.optivest.com*) and the allocation chart below, fill in the blanks.

First a few tips:

1. Start with your cash and near cash investments for conservative income and liquidity.

2. Do not allocate more than 30% to any one category or you won't be strategically diversified.

3. Start with your income requirements first, then
   add your growth asset categories.

Asset	Amount $	Yield %	Amount $	Growth %

TOTALS

Copy the form below several times so you can chart multiple alternative portfolios to review and select from.

Amount $	Total %	Amount $	Volatility %	Portfolio %

After your first attempt, look at the bottom totals. Is it enough income? Is it well diversified? What would it look like if the S&P were down 20%? Or, if interest rates climbed 300 basis points? If there were high inflation? (While you can alter your portfolio in the future, why not see what it would look like if you did not?)

The above Asset Allocation should take into consideration your present assets, priorities, goals and risk tolerances. This portfolio strategy is an optimum Asset Allocation, given your objectives and the present market environment.

However, your investment objectives *may* change and the financial markets *will* change in the future. Active portfolio management responds to these changes, as no static investment strategy can predict and protect in all economic environments.

For example, there will be times in the future when you should raise cash and add to your hard asset portfolio (gold, silver, etc.) for highly inflationary times, add to your stock portfolio during multi-year lows or create larger bond allocation during times of extremely high interest rates.

In addition, minor changes in management styles and investment instruments within an Asset Allocation will be required to optimize your returns in new financial market environments.

As you can see in the sample Asset Allocation portfolio, we strongly believe in diversification. Again, we never recommend more than a 5% position in any one real estate project, company, trust deed, Viatical, bond, etc. If something does go south, and you lose 5% of your money despite due diligence and monitoring, you should still have an *up* year.

If this appears overwhelming, start with a larger-than-normal cash allocation and ease into it. Invest in a portion of each allocation and "try it on" for a while to see how comfortable you are with the new investment vehicle. Just don't let an initial down quarter panic you into discarding a well designed plan.

LIFE CYCLES OF A PORTFOLIO

Your actual returns, particularly from real estate, will not come in neat monthly advances. In the beginning of the investment cycle, it may take a full year or more to become fully invested. During this period, your account will under-perform its targets. Stocks will also bolt up or down without any regard to your long-term performance. Bonds will be volatile and show sub-par performance due to initial commissions and accrued interest. Expect this and realize that every portfolio starts in this typically haphazard way.

The middle stage of the investment cycle is one of steady or slightly improving cash flow and more normalized growth from your stock portfolio. Your cash flow expectations should be met. But, you may feel you're falling behind in growth as there is no tangible way (short of an appraisal or offer) to measure your real estate holdings.

The mature stage of your portfolio will occur after two to four years when some of your projects go full cycle. Viaticals mature early; development projects are sold; discounted trust deeds come to term, etc. This will trigger your portfolio to out-perform for these reporting periods. Then you start all over again.

Eventually, you get into a nice rhythm with some vehicle turning over every quarter, and before you know it, your target returns are realized and sustained.

Part III

MANAGING FOR OPTIMUM SATISFACTION

...or How to Live Successfully off Your Money

ONCE YOU'VE TABULATED your initial asset allocation, you need to build a team of professional advisors who will execute it efficiently and with the highest-quality vehicles.

This segment begins by describing the pros and cons of each of your investment-advisor alternatives. Often a mucky process, this can get perplexing because everyone will be falling over each other saying they can handle your entire account. In reality, each advisor has his or her role to play. To be successful, you will need and use the talents of most of them over time.

There will then be a brief description of family offices. Envision some form of "family office," whether it's a desk in your den or a 50-man private family investment company.

Next up is a segment asking "How Much Is Enough?" (to

keep in your estate), followed by an overview on Advanced Estate Planning contributed by Garfield Langmuir-Logan, Esquire of San Juan Capistrano, California. Mr. Logan regularly establishes large estate plans for both newly acquired wealth and "Old Money," and is well respected in his field.

Appropriately enough, the final chapters of the book discuss special issues of widows and divorcées; a "What if" letter on how to leave an orderly estate; and perhaps most importantly, how to enjoy your wealth!

Chapter 18

Great Expectations:
How to Succeed as
a Private Investor

THE INTELLECTUAL EQUIPMENT for being a successful investor include: (a) knowing where you're headed with specific investment objectives; (b) giving and receiving good communication; (c) having a proper evaluation method, and (d) embracing realistic expectations.

Although we covered the development of your investment objectives, review them at least quarterly to make sure you remain comfortable with them. A down quarter, within your volatility targets, will sting, but should not be unexpected. Likewise, even if you lose money in an appropriately allocated speculation with a diversification of other speculative investments, you don't need to re-think your entire strategy. However, if you stray outside of your volatility targets, or if one of your "solid" investments went sour, something went wrong and you then need to re-evaluate your strategy and choice of advisors.

Rarely does an investment go from boom to bust without

plenty of warning. If it's a liquid investment (stock or bond) and it is not being professionally managed, you need to *always* have a *predetermined* stop loss strategy. You will probably not uncover the real reason for the drop until it is too late. Don't wait for information; sell at a 10%–15% loss and get out. You can be wrong 6 out of 10 times for every time an investment goes bust (while letting your winners run) and still come out ahead by exiting early.

CAPITAL CALLS

Making decisions about illiquid investments is more difficult and often comes with the request to pour in more money. Is this good money after bad?

Here are a few things to consider when weighing your decision:

1. Have the business or real estate project managers kept you informed along the way, or do you only hear from them when they need money?

2. Is the problem external or internal?

3. Does the situation stem from a foreseeable problem that inexperienced management didn't plan for?

4. Is there an asset that could easily be sold, such as inventory, real property, etc., to protect your investment?

5. Is your call for cash a "band-aid" or long-term fix?

6. Is this problem likely to recur?

Good Capital Calls:

1. Property taxes
2. Capital to fill genuine purchase orders in hand
3. A new tenant who needs tenant improvements
4. A new business or property acquisition
5. Funding growth, etc.

Bad Capital Calls:

1. Poor sales
2. Low occupancy
3. Lawsuit
4. Over-budget
5. Under-prepared
6. Missing pro forma numbers, etc.

If it's a "good" capital call, go ahead and pay it. If it's a "bad" capital call, first understand your risks of not paying it. If the situation is copacetic without your money and your only visible downside is dilution, don't add money. There are too many other good investments available. Why add money to a weak one if you don't have to?

The more difficult ones are the capital calls that will likely lose everything if they aren't paid. Do your homework. Most likely the person asking for the money is an optimist who, despite himself, may promise you anything to keep *his* dream alive. If you have an equity interest in income property or a first mortgage, your chances are pretty certain you'll get your money back. You can also expect a return if you are a secured creditor with an asset-based business. However, start-up businesses with *unplanned* capital calls are very iffy.

It can be a puzzlement, even on the inside, if it's going to pan out. Here are two rules of thumb:

1. Never put more than 5% of your portfolio into any single project or 25% into any single illiquid asset category.

2. Never let your unplanned capital calls exceed your original investment (or 5% allocation, ideally).

COMMUNICATION

Know your "bogey." The essential element to communicating effectively with *all* of your advisors is for everyone to know, understand and agree on a specific "bogey."

For your accountant, it might be "to pay the least amount of taxes legally possible."

For your insurance agent, it might be "securing the lowest premium for quality coverage."

For your estate planner, it might be "show me all the pros and cons of the most efficient ways to gift money to my heirs and charities," and so forth.

Your investment bogey is usually more complicated and is best defined in your "Personal Investment Charter." However, if you never want to experience a down quarter, you will have to live with a very conservative Asset Allocation that may fall short of your return targets. Measurable and realistic investment objectives that are specified and reviewed quarterly are *very* important.

Let me give you a poignant example.

In August, 1987—at the top of the market before the

"crash" in October—we invested $500,000 in the stock market for a new client. Our indicators said to sell everything on October 6: We did with a small loss.

A few weeks later, the market plummeted over 20% in a couple of days. By the end of the quarter, most stock portfolios were trimmed by 20%–25%. We went grinning into our client's office, bragging about only having a 2% loss, and were promptly fired! He was furious because CDs were paying 9%, and we lost money. Our mistake was never clarifying our "bogey" with this client up front (which should have been a stock market index).

Later that year, he sold his business for over $10 million and used another advisor. After he got shuffled around in the real world for a while, we got him back. But the overriding lesson from this client's merry-go-round was always making sure to completely understand the client's objectives, and agree that they (a) are realistic, and (b) cannot change with every pivot of the market.

Just like giving employees performance reviews, you should have a reliable and mutually agreed method to evaluate your advisors' track record.

ECONOMIC CYCLES

Keep firmly in mind that *every* investment is subject to business cycles. And yes, they still do occur.

Real estate, interest rates, stock market, foreign stock markets, gold and even CDs have attractive or atrocious cycles. While no one can predict the future, it is extremely helpful to learn from the past. "The trend is your friend" is an old Wall Street saying that is so true. But the real expertise is in identifying that trend and to know where you are in it (near the middle, start or finish).

Down cycles don't last forever, and offer the best opportunities for value-based investments. You must, however, scale in and be patient. Down cycles or "bear markets", can last a few days or 20 years (like gold). The absolute best way to leverage market cycles is to be broadly diversified, add modestly in down cycles and gradually slide back in during up cycles. If you *expect* cycles and prepare for them, you can tank your despair and greet them with an enthusiastic flair.

Even if you want to judge your advisors by their *absolute* performance (a stated return target regardless of the general markets), you must still recognize their *relative* performance as well.

Ideally, your portfolio should be balanced with inflationary (real estate, commodities, consumer business, etc.) and deflationary (bonds, most stocks, etc.) investments that will keep you centered in most environments.

I repeat "most" because virtually everything went down during the great depression of the 1820s, the debt repudiation of the 1840s, the pre- and post-Civil War depressions of the 1850s and 1870s, the worldwide depression of the 1890s, post-World War I depression of the 1930s and a lot of garden variety recessions in between.

In the last 70 years, we have been very fortunate not to have a general depression. But regional depressions do occur. Two relatively fresh ones were the "oil depression" in Texas in the mid-1980s and the "real estate depression" in California in the early 1990s. But these passed and eventually were followed by boom times.

Again, the key is to be mindful that there will be future times when outside forces can temporarily ruin a given market. Simply prepare for it by broad diversification and by giving yourself some safety margin (cash and borrowing power) to exploit weak markets.

Help protect yourself by having a clear investment charter written and reviewed often with your advisors, by diversifying broadly, by setting stop loss limits, and by keeping heads up for the swings in market cycles.

One other caveat: I just wish I could give you 10 pointers on how to freeze your emotions as well. I know it's difficult, as I have a much easier time being objective and disciplined with my client's money than with my own. The simplest and best way is to jointly agree with your advisors on the ground rules and let them implement your marching orders in good conscience on your behalf.

Chapter 19

Whom Do I Turn To?

(Investment Advisor Alternatives)

ALTHOUGH I HAVE a built-in bias from my past experiences within the industry, I also have that special insider's insight and un-politicized freedom to convey the realities of the various advisor alternatives.

In the past, I was a leading stockbroker at a large Wall Street firm (Smith Barney); co-owned a small NASD broker/dealer (Hagerty, Van Mourick & Logan); wrote a stock market newsletter (OPTIVEST); managed stock portfolios (Smith Barney and OPTIVEST); performed traditional financial planning, and sold investment insurance (Smith Barney/OPTIVEST).

Although I have not worked at a large money management company, bank or trust company, I know their strengths and weaknesses as I have taken clients from (and lost clients to) them over the years. With that disclaimer out of the way, I do have an objective perspective to judge the kinds of services you can expect from the variety of financial advisors.

LARGE BROKERAGE FIRMS

Almost all large investors will find a need for a top-notch relationship with a big wire house. While there will continue to be mergers and blurred lines among brokerage firms and banks, some of the most sophisticated financial securities transactions are conducted at these firms. You should specifically try for a comfortable relationship with a top broker from Merrill Lynch, Salomon Smith Barney, Goldman Sachs or Morgan Stanley. DLJ, Hambrecht & Quist, and Robertson Stephens are also superb for OTC stock issues. However, these broker/dealers are best at transaction business and should be used mostly for that purpose.

When you are a broker at a large firm, you are judged internally by one criterion: your annual gross commissions (sometimes I felt it was tattooed across my forehead!). The accounts that lose money are the only client performance charts that are reviewed by management. It's strictly a commission/fee-oriented world with scant accountability toward performance. To be completely fair, they *want* to do well for you so you'll do more business, as it requires a lot of overhead and marketing effort to constantly open new accounts.

Assess these considerations regarding large brokerage firms:

Strengths—large stock & bond research departments; familiarity with large transactions; complicated insider trading issues; newest stock tax strategies; mergers and acquisitions; specialty products like syndications; venture capital deals; and exchange funds;

Weaknesses—work for the firm, not clients; limited diversification potential into non-financial vehicles; too many clients to serve limits personal attention (I had 1,200 accounts at Smith Barney); seldom ever issue a sell recommendation.

One overriding thought: Do not give full discretion to a commissioned salesman. They can't help themselves. Save that for the professional money managers.

SMALL BROKERAGE FIRMS

Some of the very best brokers have shed their alignments with big brokers and repositioned themselves as principals in their own small broker/dealer boutique agencies for flexibility and higher earnings potential.

Then again, some of the big brokerage firms' washouts also wind up in small broker/dealers because no other big broker will hire them. It'll be relatively easy to determine which one you are dealing with after some basic legwork with the N.A.S.D. or local professionals (accountants and lawyers). In the meantime, you are sufficiently tipped off: This could be the best or the worst place for a large investor.

Let's assume you're working with a reputable small firm and broker. You should be able to receive most basic financial products and services of a large firm, but with a higher degree of personal attention. They won't have large proprietary syndications, new offerings, analysts (though they'll probably have access to some large firm's research) or in-house legal and tax experts. But they will have the same S.I.P.C. and additional insurance of most big firms and can be more flexible on commission rates. The greatest possible advantage would be working with a superstar advisor and his/her ability to tap into *local* real estate and business deals.

Consider these characteristics:

Strengths—more personalized service; local deals; stocks; bonds; mutual funds; and relationships with money managers;

Weaknesses—less exposure to new and large syndications/ offerings; usually no in-house legal/tax experts; a bias toward stocks and loaded mutual funds; and minimal business capitalization.

You can research your small broker/dealer on the Internet by going to the N.A.S.D. website at *www.nasd.com* and making sure they're not engaged in ongoing battles with client complaints.

PRIVATE BANKING AND TRUST COMPANIES

This is where big money used to park. And today private banking and trust companies still meet the needs of many very wealthy people. They are discreet, oriented toward client performance, fee-based and have the "safety" of a large institution.

Most large U.S. and European banks have a private banking division to manage money for $5 million and larger accounts. They are accustomed to multi-generational and estate planning issues. They can also immediately assist you with personal credit lines and banking needs (such as delivering $10,000 in cash on a Sunday afternoon). The largest trust companies have similar services and are sometimes extensions of a major client's initial full-service family office.

Unfortunately, all this service usually arrives with mediocre performance and an overall lack of consumerism. You will basically receive their in-house stock management (which will attempt to mirror the S&P 500) and enough muni bonds to support your income needs. Sometimes they will show you a private real estate transaction, but they seldom are players who get to pick and choose from a large "deal flow." They are best suited for managing the funds of widows and minors or large multi-beneficiary trusts.

However, if you prefer to have your personal accounting performed by a Big Five firm, don't keep more than $100,000 at any given bank; if you have conservative performance expectations, you might feel cozy here. Our favorites are Bank of America, Mellon Bank, Credit Sussie and Northern Trust Company.

Weigh their characteristics:

Strengths—fee-based institutional management; country-club-like banking services; and big institutional security;

Weaknesses—mediocre performance; lack of diversification; constant turnover of account representatives; and minimal proactive investment action.

Lastly, do not name a bank or trust company (or any big institution) as a trustee or co-trustee on a family trust. Such an institution will become almost impossible to fire in the future without the heirs going to court. There is much cleaner and smoother handling with a family member, friend or even an attorney as a trustee.

TRADITIONAL MONEY MANAGERS

These are mostly large stock-managers who supervise individual accounts with discretion for a fee (not commission).

Although there are over 2,000 such managers in the U.S., only about 25% beat the S&P in any given year.

Most of the managers (many of whom also manage mutual funds) are either growth or value oriented; top down (directed by economic cycles) or bottom up (individual company selection driven); and specialize in large cap or small cap companies. In addition, there are a number of specialty styles like arbitrage, rising dividend, international and covered call writing. Each management style has its day in the sun with its respective methodologies in favor for a few months to a few years. But no style works in all market environments.

The fine art of selecting money managers is terribly tricky. Fundamentally, if you choose a narrow management style (small cap value, for example), you will significantly underperform or over-perform the big indexes in a given year. If you choose a broad style or a combination of many money managers, you will simply mirror the big indexes. Choosing a particular manager within a style is also important. But don't get discouraged. There are a lot of good stock managers to choose from.

Yet a traditional money manager is only part of your needs. They don't diversify beyond stocks and bonds; don't (or shouldn't) change management styles with the changing economy; don't offer personal services; and are not good general investment counselors.

Consider these points:

Strengths—focused fee-based stock and bond management; only require quarterly monitoring; and low fee structure (cheaper than mutual funds for large accounts);

Weaknesses—minimal non-stock diversification; no portfolio customization; and a lack of expertise outside of their specific discipline.

FINANCIAL PLANNERS

Financial planners (fee and/or commission) help families objectively evaluate their current financial condition, create plans for saving for your children's education, and plot a path for retirement and estate tax.

These initial financial plans cost $1,500 to $15,000, are usually pretty complete and use computer software for their calculations. The truth is, most financial plans are covered in dust. Less than half are ever implemented, and few of those reach full execution. While future projections are never accurate (assuming you understand and believe the basic premise of the future estimates), they are still very helpful in planning your future.

Most solutions to the financial planner's proposal are narrow: Mutual funds and life insurance are the typical background of the majority. Although these are excellent tools for small investors for saving for the future, they are often woefully inadequate for the diversification needs of larger accounts (over $1 million).

Like stockbrokers, most good financial planners have hundreds, or in some cases, thousands of clients. They are prioritized into A, B and C accounts and receive attention on the same scale. Unfortunately, even an A account will not receive undiluted personal attention. Face-to-face meetings usually occur annually.

Here are the pros and cons:

Strengths—broader-based objective advice; financial plans for future; customized portfolios; and knowledgeable in estate-planning issues and insurance needs;

Weaknesses—usually seek "up-and-comers," not multi-million dollar accounts; top heavy with mutual fund and insurance products; and too many accounts.

Look for a C.F.P. (Certified Financial Planner) license and a background beyond a career steeped in insurance.

INVESTMENT ADVISORS
(A one-minute commercial)

There are a few firms, like ours, that cater exclusively to large accounts. We have successfully woven together the strengths of the small broker/dealer, the fee-based financial advisor and private banking with the look and feel of a family office for multiple clients.

We fully recognize the attributes of private banks, large brokerage firms and traditional money managers; introduce our clients to their services; and manage their activity. We work intensely for a small number of clients. By developing close relationships with the best specialists at the leading real estate, venture capital, and stock and bond firms, we can coordinate and manage a very broad range of investments. Our stable of support also extends to the top tax, legal, estate planning and insurance professionals in our community. For more in-depth information, please visit our website at *www.optivestinc.com*.

An honest evaluation:

Strengths—very personal service and customized portfolios; access to virtually all investment vehicles; understanding of personal and emotional issues of wealthy families; and congenial investment counseling;

Weaknesses—limited number of accounts; more expensive than some advisors; lack of in-house specialists; limited expertise in mutual funds; and defy standard cookie-cutter financial planning.

Once you've narrowed down the type of advisor that best suits your needs, you still must select a firm and a person. My suggestion, since most of the firms have similar capabilities, is look for the best individual you can find first. Your ultimate performance will have more to do with that person's judgment and experience than what name is on the letterhead. Start with referrals from well-respected friends, business associates and related professionals (CPAs and lawyers).

Look for these characteristics in an advisor:

Capabilities—Does the advisor have the background, experience and education necessary to make wise decisions on your large account? Look for a senior level person that has advised the firm's biggest accounts for at least 10 years.

Resources—Does the advisor have access to a wide range of information, research, deal flow, networking and other tools to use on your behalf? Ask to see the breadth of their investment options and resources.

Integrity—Will the advisor truly work as *your* advocate, keeping your agenda ahead of the firm's and his own self-interest? Look for someone that's deeply established in their community and talk to current long-term clients.

You need an advisor that meets all three requirements. Two out of three will not work. Even if he's capable and has the resources, you still have to be able to trust him. If you can trust him and he's capable, but has limited resources, it won't work either. If he has high integrity and plentiful resources, but lacks experience working with big accounts, you will also suffer. You will need all three characteristics in an advisor: Don't settle for less. The time you spend searching out a great advisor will be richly rewarded.

Chapter 20

Getting the Most out of Your Advisor

(Or, Never Having a Communications Breakdown)

Y<small>OU DESERVE AT</small> a minimum (and have a right to demand) accurate and timely information regarding your investments.

Traditionally, such reporting is done quarterly, which may suit some if everything is sailing along as planned. If not, you need to know promptly. My friend Richard Felix who was the President of Azusa Pacific University from 1990 to 2000, has a great streamlined policy: *No surprises, bad news first, full disclosure.*

You probably will have to train your advisors, but do let them know what your communication expectations are up front. With e-mail, instant messaging, phones, pagers, Palm Pilots and faxes, there is absolutely no reason you should ever be in the dark. After you are comfortable with the steady progress of your investments, you can skim reports—but always insist on keeping them coming.

For your lead advisor(s), I recommend a formal quarterly meeting with a set agenda. It should include your quarterly expectations, what went right and wrong, the economic climate period, implementation of changes, and a full accounting of your portfolio holdings.

This accounting should include a year-to-date performance overall and by each investment, not just a current portfolio appraisal. You should also receive year-to-date realized gains and losses, income and expenses, and unrealized gains to help your accountant plan your taxes. Charts are helpful, but not necessary.

Your quarterly meeting should also devote time to *anticipated* activity and expected results from the next quarter (which you will probably be halfway through by the time of the meeting). Make sure you are in a comfort zone with each investment or have a plan of action if certain benchmarks are not met.

The single most important agenda item is a bottom line, crystal clear, mutual understanding of what the bogey is (and it cannot change each quarter). If the advisor's bogey is to beat the relative performance of an index (like the S&P 500), don't expect him to outperform CDs if the market goes down.

Kick the bogey around often and change it if you must. But keep it realistic. Twice the return of the S&P 500 without volatility is a moonbeam. Make it obtainable within a set time frame.

Chapter 21

Family Offices

(The Ultimate Suite Life)

MAYBE YOU'VE COME full circle, from the garage where you tinkered with that invention, to the den where you're embarking on managing the empire from the family office.

Family offices are a status symbol for the wealthy, but in reality can mean anything. They can range from keeping track of mutual funds on your computer to a 50-person office with in-house legal and accounting staff as well as an active stock, bond and real estate management matrix with a strategic investment committee.

You will probably want something in-between and will have to decide what to keep "in-house" and what to "outsource." Let's look at some investor profiles and their in-house options.

ACTIVE INVESTOR

If you enjoy (and can afford) to spend your days watching the financial markets, you can manage any size portfolio of stocks, bonds and mutual funds from a home PC. However, unless you can consistently beat the stock market indexes, let a professional pick your stocks (see chapter 9, "The Stock Market"). Otherwise, you will probably get sub-par performances *and* spend all day doing it. On the other hand, with a mutual fund or stock manager doing the nitty-gritty of intraday stock management, everything else can be monitored daily or weekly.

To be truly successful on your own, you need reams of current and historical information as well as a network of contacts to glean and bounce ideas and information. Although the Internet has an endless depth of information, it is shallow on strategic thinking.

If you are managing your life savings and depend on it for your income, you must consider it a full time job and apply yourself accordingly. Read books, newsletters, newspapers, magazines, and attend seminars and trade shows. Instill a disciplined investment system to execute a buy, hold or sell with confidence. Stick with your system and monitor your progress closely. The most difficult aspect of managing your own money is keeping your emotions in check while taking your losses early.

IN-HOUSE EXPERT

If you can relinquish control, the next level of a family office is to hire an in-house expert as the aforementioned active investor. This expert will work full-time for the family, usually on a salary and performance bonus.

Often such an expert will emerge from an existing relationship with your accountant, stockbroker, financial planner or insurance agent. Regardless of their previous profession, the expert will come on board with his or her industry biases toward investing philosophy and products. This may sound attractive in theory and I have seen some successes with this type of arrangement. But most often, people willing to leave their industry for a one-client job are washouts on their way out anyway.

You'll get what you pay for here. A modest salary hires a rookie whose learning curve will be on your dime. A top salary can hire a lot of experience but is a risky move for a professional (because if it doesn't work out, he or she may have to start over in their industry without a book of clients).

The best source of in-house experts comes right from within your own company or family. Train them in the investment areas you want to emphasize. Dish out a little at a time and monitor the results closely. In most cases, the success rate will be greater if your expert can establish a network of contacts with financial industry experts and/or "partner" with outside management for specific tasks like stock or real estate.

This in-house expert will require a real office and perhaps some support staff. To properly equip a qualified professional to manage your investments in-house could cost hundreds of thousands of dollars. This type of arrangement works best on estates in excess of $50 million. But remember, you will still have to pay *outside* legal, accounting and most likely management fees. The most cost-effective way to kick-start an in-house expert is by creating a division in your existing family business and utilizing current office space and staff.

REAL FAMILY OFFICES

The largest "household name" estates have real family offices. These are efficient for the Forbes 400 families, as they look and act like small investment companies (without the salesmen). They can attract top talent and handle all aspects of the family's financial, legal and tax needs from within.

Instead of searching for ideal investments, the top opportunities come to them first. If you truly have the resources to consider this option, visit established family offices and private banking operations. But don't do it alone. Pick an advisory board of experts to help you with the design, and form a strategic investment committee.

OPTIVEST

OPTIVEST was formed in 1987 to efficiently act like a surrogate family office for a small group of wealthy investors. We personally perform all the investment functions and work closely with outside accountants and attorneys who are also specialists in the financial affairs of wealthy clients.

Since we only work with clients who have similar financial objectives—moderate to moderately aggressive—we have tremendous economy of scale and client synergy.

Chapter 22

How Much Is Enough?

T HE TYPICAL ANSWER from my clients is "just a little bit more." But at some point, your wealth accumulation crosses a line where it becomes more for your heirs and charities than your own personal needs. This is a highly subjective question and open to much personal debate. Let me give some practical guidelines.

First and foremost, every dollar earned in your estate is worth only 45 cents to your heirs. If you can transfer your funds into their name(s) now, every dollar of future growth is theirs without estate tax.

Secondly, consider gifting now so you can *enjoy* watching your beneficiaries use it. You can also control how they spend it (educational trust, etc.) or let them learn (and you can teach) as they go. But dying with a huge estate is meaningless if you care about your beneficiaries.

Gifting now will require creating additional trusts such as CRTs, foundations, QPRT, etc., but will save you potentially hundreds of thousands in items like insurance premiums. Place your children on these boards, teach them the rules and art of investment, and give them responsibilities. You have an increased opportunity to perpetuate your family values if you get your heirs involved before you pass on.

Let's say you agree that some form of your estate should/could go to your beneficiaries now. But how much? Let's look at your personal needs first.

If your children are on their own (out of college), you have funds set aside for them, and a "paid for" home(s) that reflect your lifestyle, you only need 3 times the value of these homes in cash-flow investments to retire comfortably.

As an example, if a couple has a $2 million debt-free home, they could reasonably retire on $6 million in income investments ($480,000 per year @8% pre-tax). You could probably live on 66% of the income and save for the future. I have seen this formula work quite well on $200,000 homes and $20 million homes. If you have 3 times the value of your homes invested (as I outlined in this book), you will have more than enough to live on for the rest of your life.

How much you give away above this amount is up to you. It is unlikely, however, you will ever use it for your own benefit. You will be surprised and quite delighted at the joy it will bring to see your heirs and charities enriching lives responsibly because of your ongoing generosity.

At the same time, don't extinguish your children's ambitions or desires to become financially independent. There is an inverse effect of giving children too much money and their ability/desire to be self-sufficient.

We had one client who sent his daughter to college with a new BMW, put her in an expensive condo and gave her a generous clothing allowance. When she graduated, she could not land a job that would pay enough to maintain her cushy lifestyle. So her parents decided to help her further along until she got on her own. She's now in her mid-30s and still leaning on her parents for income.

In lieu of financing this learned dependency, teach your children early to budget their money. Give them money-matching incentives to work toward a car or first home. Help fund their IRAs or children's education fund, treat them to nice vacations and gifts, make annual contributions to reduce their mortgages, but DO NOT provide their daily bread.

Leave them that dignity and they will become self-sufficient and productive adults.

Chapter 23

A Few Choice Words
About Insurance

I CANNOT TELL a lie. I hate insurance. Yet I have to admit I've worked with enough widows (who were the recipients of a large policy) to know what a benefit it can be if your net worth won't support your spouse's lifestyle, especially if it's conservatively invested.

But at some point in your net worth, you don't need insurance for your spouse to continue to be financially comfortable. The best usage of term insurance is to protect a temporary drop of income for a predetermined length of time. If you died today, what people or entities (if any) would suffer from your lack of *earned* income? If you have some, insure that stream of income for the necessary period of time. However, if your investment assets already provide enough income for your household needs (or can be rearranged to do so), don't buy insurance for your spouse.

Insurance for your estate plan is completely different. First determine how much you and your spouse really need in your estate for your lifestyle (see chapter 22 on "How Much Is Enough?"). Once you've got that figure in mind, meet with your estate planning lawyer to gift the rest to your children and/or charities. You can retain control if you wish, but get it out of your taxable estate. With qualified personal residence trusts, family partnerships, creative title transfers, etc., you can probably gift as much as you want over time.

You will perhaps still pass on with a taxable estate, but it will be much smaller (so will the estate tax). Ask yourself, "Is this money for my heirs?" If you want to leave more, decide how much more they will really get if you pay insurance premiums versus gifting that money today to invest themselves.

Just because you will potentially owe a certain dollar amount of estate tax, it doesn't necessarily translate into how much insurance to buy. The ultimate question is how much do you want to leave your heirs at your (and your spouse's) death versus giving it to them now (or sacrificing future income for a larger future lump sum).

Do not let an insurance person tell you how much insurance you should leave your heirs. Do your estate planning and gifting and then determine the total amount they receive at death. If it's less than your present estate, purchase that much of permanent (whole life) insurance. Otherwise, skip the insurance and give more today. There's no rational reason to die with as large of an estate as you can build.

Let me give you an example.

If a couple has a current estate (net worth) of $20 million, live comfortably in a $2 million home(s), and have grown children who are self-sufficient, my formula of 3 times their free-and-clear house (which reflects their lifestyle) suggests this couple only needs income from about $6 million to support their current and inflation-protected future lifestyle

($480,000/year of tax-free income in munis and real estate).

This leaves $12 million of assets they probably don't need to affect their lifestyle. Who or what *could* benefit from that money today or in the future? You can creatively gift over time most if not all of that $12 million. This money will continue to grow (invested as you wish), but out of your taxable estate. Your beneficiaries can get the income (or you can in some cases), and the principal can go to them at some opportune day in the future. Plus, you get the real joy of gifting it today and watching your loved ones benefit.

You could even buy annuities and get a reverse mortgage to end up dying without an estate. This would create an abundant cash flow during your lifetime to use as you see fit or gift even more. If you still want to leave your heirs more money at death, buy insurance. But first consider the alternative ways to benefit your heirs and use insurance to fund the balance.

Notice I have not written about insurance as an investment vehicle. While deferred annuities have a tax deferral aspect, I believe you are better served in other investment vehicles. I've never met (or heard of) anyone becoming wealthy by investing in insurance products. Modest performance, fees and lack of flexibility more than offset their tax advantages.

Chapter 24

Advanced Estate Planning

by Garfield Langmuir-Logan, Esquire

W HILE THERE ARE many vehicles that can protect assets for the individual and for his or her heirs, in almost every case, you will be better served by doing Advanced Estate and Tax Planning *before* the sale of your company.

Since each situation will have differences, the attorney and client need to review the following:

1. Value of assets
2. Client concerns about wealth transfer
3. Client estimate of funds to retain in estate
4. Client future income needs
5. Client charities
6. Client children as part of business
7. Client control

Let's review an actual client case to get an understanding and feel of the various Advanced Estate-Planning vehicles.

A client arrived with 95% of his estate concentrated in stock in one very successful communications industry giant. The value of the stock had appreciated to a truly extraordinary level. Although impressive, it was also highly risky as there was no diversification of the assets.

While the temptation to diversify was immediate, the problem with selling a stock that was bought at less than 1% of the current value was the triggering of a huge capital gains liability, even at the long-term reduced capital gains rate.

In this case, the basics needed to be covered first.

These included:

1. A Revocable Living Trust (RLT)
2. Last Will and Testament (Will)
3. Durable Power of Attorney for Property Management (DPAPM)
4. Durable Power of Attorney for Health Care (DPAHC)

(California allows the DPAHC by statute. However, in many states, the closest vehicle would be a Living Will. For this chapter, I will refer to either or both the DPAHC and a Living Will with the one designation of DPAHC.)

Although I assume most people have these estate planning documents, that assumption was false in this case.

Furthermore, if these documents were prepared prior to the estate having a net value of $1.5 million, then the client would quite possibly need the RLT to be amended and restated with additional protection provisions.

The balance of the solution was developed in multiple layers.

First, a Charitable Remainder Trust (CRT) and an Irrevocable Life Insurance Trust (ILIT) were created. About 20% of the client's total shares was transferred into a CRT for the benefit of the Grantor.

Only after the transfer of shares were the shares then used to create an income stream to the Grantor. In this case it was through the optioning of shares. In most cases, the shares would be sold and reinvested in income-producing investments.

Keep in mind that in these instances, while the CRT will not pay capital gains tax on the disposition of the highly appreciated stock (or any income tax for that matter), income tax needs to be paid by the income beneficiary of the CRT upon receipt of the CRT distributions.

The income beneficiary of the CRT (who in this case is also the Grantor and the Trustee) then had an income to meet income requirements and to provide for sufficient gifting funds to be paid to the Trustee of the ILIT. The ILIT then purchased an insurance policy on the life of the Grantor in an amount approximately equal to the value of the shares gifted to the CRT.

These actions provided for wealth replacement to the Grantor's heirs outside the Grantor's estate at approximately the same time that the income to the Grantor ceased—at Grantor's death—from the CRT. The total value of the CRT to a qualified charity of the Grantor's choosing was then paid out and a similar amount was paid to the heirs from the insurance policy tax-free.

At the same time, a Family Limited Partnership (FLP) was created. Since a small portion of the client's net assets are held in two separate businesses, those assets, along with several properties owned by the client and a block of stocks, were all used to create the FLP.

The client then became general partner and his RLT became the primary limited partner. Each of his children then purchased (through a promissory note to the RLT) a 1% interest in the FLP. An appraisal and discount valuation was obtained by a qualified business appraiser to validate the value of the purchase interest. This allowed him to gift up to 40% more of his assets without an estate tax.

(As you can tell, this can become quite complicated, but it is prudent to at least be aware of the multiple layers that need to be applied for significant tax reductions.)

The next phase for this particular client was the creation of a separate CRT for each of his children who are all adults. Each child is the income beneficiary. Simultaneously, an ILIT was prepared for each child's spouse and the Grantor's grandchildren to replace the CRT income stream on the death of the Grantor's child. These ILITs were funded initially with a cash gift from the Grantor and will receive ongoing gifts from the Trustor through cash, FLP interest or a direct gift of stock. The CRTs (for the children's benefit) were funded with a gift of stock, which like the initial CRT, has optioned the stock.

After that, a Grandchild Generation Skip Transfer Tax Trust (GST) was created for each of the client's grandchildren. The GST Trusts were funded with a gift with interest in the FLP equal to the annual exclusion gift of $10,000, after the discount valuation and the FLP had been determined. In this case, a discount for marketability and lack of control were factored to 22%, allowing a transfer of approximately $12,820 worth of assets to each GST Trust. This was important inasmuch as the client had already utilized all of his Applicable Exclusion Amount (formerly known as the Unified Credit).

In this case, the client decided in the end not to create a Qualified Personal Residence Trust (QPRT) at that time since the home's value was worth less than 1% of the overall net estate value, and since the client planned to purchase an additional home within the next couple of years which will have a much higher value. But a QPRT can transfer your residence to your heirs over a period of years with highly reduced or complete elimination of estate tax.

The good news was that the client was able to lower his future estate tax bill by 65%! This results in tens of millions of dollars going to the heirs and charity instead of the government. It is definitely worth taking time to explore the benefits you might achieve.

CAPSULE SUMMARIES OF ESTATE VEHICLES

The following are descriptions of the most common uses and individual nuances of the Advanced Estate Planning vehicles we can create for clients. These descriptions are by no means complete, but will provide you with the basic parameters of each.

IRREVOCABLE LIFE INSURANCE TRUST (ILIT)

If the Living Trust, Will and Durable Power of Attorney (both for health care purposes and for property management purposes) make up the "framework" of estate planning, an ILIT is equivalent to its "walls" and necessary "fixtures."

An ILIT is often used to provide an infusion of cash (from the life insurance policy payment) at your death (outside of your estate) to your beneficiaries. This becomes especially important in the larger estate because it provides a reasonably quick source of income. This income can be used to pay estate taxes or other debts without having to liquidate assets that may not be easily liquidated (or would be liquidated at a loss under current timing or circumstances).

Once the cash is received from the policy liquidation, the Trustee could loan cash to the estate through a secured loan agreement or deed of trust. Alternately, the Trustee could buy one or more of the estate's assets with cash. Ultimately the beneficiaries of the ILIT will receive these assets.

During the Trustor's lifetime, an ILIT can be funded by using the client's annual exclusion gifts ($10,000 per donee from a donor). This process requires that beneficiaries of the trust (if written properly, this can also include contingent beneficiaries) receive a withdrawal right for a period of time. "Crummy Notices" are sent to all applicable beneficiaries that a gift has been made to the ILIT and their portion of the gift is $X. They have a right to withdraw this portion from the ILIT for X number of days. This is determined by the terms of the ILIT but should be at least 15 days; most attorneys make it from 30 to 60 days.

The Trustee has already begun the process of purchasing a life insurance policy or of transferring an existing policy. Please note that if you transfer an existing policy, the insured must live for three years after the transfer has been completed by the insurance company (which sometimes can take as long as 6 to 9 months to complete).

Once the life insurance policy is owned by the ILIT, then an annual contribution can be made to the Trust. Annual contributions can be made by utilizing the annual $10,000 gift exemptions.

The ILIT is best prepared by an attorney since wording in an ILIT must meet very specific criteria to qualify and comply with the tax code. Initial—and ongoing gifting to the trust— also needs to be documented and Crummy Notices sent with each new gift.

GRANDCHILD GENERATION SKIP TRANSFER TAX TRUST (GST TRUST)

A GST Trust is a specialized irrevocable trust which provides for gifting to the client's grandchildren. This trust is prepared to direct an exemption of $1 million from the generation skip transfer tax. The generation skip transfer tax is a minimum two-tiered tax to any portion of the estate which skips a generation in gifting. Also note that a gift to someone who is not a descendant, but who is X-years (per generation level) younger than you, also falls under this generation transfer tax.

To put it in its simplest terms, the transfer of your estate, after an allowance for lifetime exclusions, is currently taxed at 55% estate tax by the federal government (which, in most states, is the full amount owed, although some have an additional state inheritance tax). If the gift is not made to the children or that level generation (up or down) but instead is made at an additional level generation (i.e. grandchildren), then the remaining estate after the initial 55% tax is taxed at another 55%! A GST Trust can avoid this painful double taxation.

DYNASTY (PERPETUAL) TRUST

This is a continuing form of the aforementioned GST Trust. It is generally used in VERY large estates and is extremely difficult to prepare. Ultimately, it is a trust that might be valid for more than a century, and in these fast-paced times, it is difficult to know how to properly plan for division and disposition of the trust assets.

QUALIFIED PERSONAL RESIDENCE TRUST (QPRT)

This is a trust that's defined under a specific section of the Internal Revenue Code. It allows for the transfer of the

Trustor's personal residence (and up to one vacation home per person) to the Trustor's beneficiary. Although a complicated trust, the gift of the property to the QPRT is made, but the Trustor remains the Trustee and beneficiary until the end of the trust term. The longer the trust term, the higher the discount to the value of the property.

This is an excellent vehicle for people in their mid-50s to late 60s who have superb health and a genetic history of long life.

There are, however, some risks in the QPRT. If the Trustor outlives the trust term, the property is transferred at the end of the trust term to ownership by the ultimate beneficiaries of the QPRT (usually the Trustor's children). It is conceivable the beneficiaries may want to rent the property to the Trustor for reasonable market value. If the estate is still substantial, then that would allow for further transfer of the estate to the beneficiaries. Yet it is also possible the beneficiaries may elect to sell the property and take the proceeds. This could occur when the Trustor may not want to move. Plus, there are provisions in the tax code which preclude the Trustor from purchasing the home at the end of the term. You need to be able to trust your beneficiaries.

A secondary risk is if the Trustor does not live until at least the final year of the trust. If that happens, the property reverts to the Trustor's estate and any gift tax that may have been paid because of the transfer is credited to the estate. Except for the cost of the preparation and administration of the QPRT, everything now remains as it was before the creation of the document.

FOREIGN ASSET PROTECTION TRUST (APT)

This is a trust with some significant problems and liability to the attorney. Many estate-planning attorneys will not prepare an APT. Those who do may charge very high fees (often ranging from $25,000 to $100,000). The ongoing fees with the foreign trust company often tend to be very high as well ($10,000 or more per year). The APT is a good vehicle for someone who is not a U.S. citizen and who has income from outside the U.S., and therefore does not have any federal taxes on that income or someone who is the likely target for litigation.

Assets put in an APT would need to be unattachable by a court in the U.S. To put ownership of a piece of real property located in the United States into an APT will probably not provide any real protection from the property being attached, since the court would be able to take action on or against the property. But financial securities, even managed accounts, can be placed into an APT.

CHARITABLE REMAINDER TRUST (CRT) AND CHARITABLE LEAD TRUST

As previously discussed, please refer to chapter 2, "Before Signing the Letter of Intent."

FAMILY LIMITED LIABILITY ENTITY (LP or LLC) OR FAMILY LIMITED PARTNERSHIP (FLP)

Again, please refer to chapter 2, "Before Signing the Letter of Intent."

Garfield Langmuir-Logan, Esq.

Chapter 25

Sensitive Services for Widows and Divorcées

OVER THE YEARS, I have assisted a number of women from ages 30 through 80 with unique problems and issues arising from the death or divorce of their wealthy husbands.

Oftentimes, these women were not actively involved in either the day-to-day management of their household money or the management of their investments. While they may have considerable assets to meet their financial requirements, they're starting from a handicapped point of view, both from an educational standpoint as well as an emotional one. This "mental freeze" often leads to either cash hoarding (as opposed to investing) or being manipulated by a commissioned salesman.

If you are a husband reading this right now, I heartily encourage you to begin including your wife in your financial affairs and immediately write an "Open if" letter as described in the following chapter. Even if your wife is disinterested, be insistent and have her attend some key meetings with your advisors. Or, at the very least, give her a master overview of your issues and courses of action. The goal would be to make sure she could "carry on" if you weren't around.

If you are a recent widow or divorcée reading this, I truly empathize with you. Besides managing your grief, you are trying to deal with monumental changes in your life and are facing a growing list of potentially unfamiliar monetary choices. Let me offer a few quick suggestions.

1. Take it slowly. Get to know your present bankers, lawyers, accountants and financial advisors. Ask them to present only the most pressing items to you; i.e., decisions that have to be made within 60 days. If, for any reason, you don't feel at all comfortable with an advisor, make a change. Get a fresh referral from your most trusted advisor or family friend who would most likely know.

2. Choose a lead advisor who understands your big picture and can coordinate with your other advisors to work as a team.

3. Within 180 days, *schedule 1- to 2-hour separate meetings* with your estate planning attorney and each advisor on your investments (stock manager, real estate manager, etc.). Have each explain in detail their methodology, philosophy and track record, etc. They're talking about your funds, so ask questions until you are completely satisfied. You don't need to learn how they run their businesses, but you do need to fundamentally understand what they're doing to be on the alert for specific risks that could occur.

4. Deposit all of your income directly into a bank or brokerage money market account that can provide you with detailed accounting. Ask your accountant to give you an estimated monthly *after-tax* income figure and have that amount deposited into your household bank account at the beginning of each month. Since your bills normally arrive monthly, this way you can count on an even monthly "pay check" even if your income actually comes in quarterly or semi-annually.

5. Now—with your monthly pay check—*establish a rough budget*. Look through the last six months of household expenses and jot down what you expect to pay each month. Be sure to budget for semi-annual payments like insurance and taxes. If you need help, don't put it off or be shy about it. Ask a trusted friend, family member or financial advisor to start it for you or review it. You need to understand your monthly expenses and stay on top of them so they won't begin to overwhelm you.

6. There will be *times when you may have to tap into your principal* to pay monthly expenses, unexpected expenses or large expenditures such as trips or cars. That's fine, but don't do it blindly.

7. At some point in the first year, you'll want to *make short- to intermediate-term lifestyle decisions*. Do you want to maintain the house or

move to a smaller residence? That's usually the biggest question you'll be facing. But, again, take it slowly. It's best to stay in your larger residence for a longer period than to move too hastily to a wrong location.

Decisions made in haste often lead to waste. Again, take it slowly and ease your way through all the questions you'll be facing.

Chapter 26

An "Open if" Letter
to Your Spouse

IN MY DESK drawer there's a handwritten envelope with the words "Trish, Open if..."

The letter inside the envelope contains practical information for my spouse (and office manager) if perchance I didn't make it back from one of my climbing adventures. With step-by-step guidance, the letter addresses many of the issues my wife would have to face within the first 60 days.

Several of my clients have requested guidance for drafting a similar letter to their spouses to help them settle their business and financial affairs and develop a basic plan for living without the breadwinner.

The hour you spend drafting an "Open if" letter could save your spouse months of confusion and heartache at a time when he or she is least able to cope emotionally, let alone financially. The letter does not answer every question your spouse will have, but it will help with the initial priority issues and how to regroup financially.

The following are simple suggestions based on the contents of my letter. Although this can be uncomfortable, once you overcome your mortality you will be completely at ease.

Introduction

Consider starting with an apology for your untimely passing, then describe the purpose of this letter; i.e., helping your spouse and your children with some of the immediate practical problems they will soon be facing.

First Week

1. **Funeral arrangements**—If you have a particular desire, such as cremation, state it here. If you don't, offer some general suggestions, like "...keep it simple: Please don't spend thousands on a velvet coffin," etc.

2. **Initial Finances**—Every family is unique but here are some ideas to include:

   Line of Credits/Home Equity Lines—Draw them out immediately. They can be used for basic living expenses until the insurance money comes in. They may also be canceled by the bank soon because of reduced family earnings.

   Near Term Income—Tell your spouse how to collect any earned income that you may not have received. It might be as simple as contacting a coworker or business partner. Try to be specific when describing people to call.

3. **Life Insurance**—Describe your policy; where it is and whom to contact to file a claim. Let your spouse know it is tax-free and you will tell them later in the letter what should be done with it.

4. **Identify an Advocate**—Give your spouse suggestions on whom she or he can turn to for help with initial family affairs. This could be your best friend, neighbor, golfing buddy, an in-law, business partner, etc. This trusted person can handle immediate problems and eventually help create a household budget, negotiate the sale of the business or property, and initiate interaction with your spouse's future financial advisor.

5. **Records**—Spell out where to find financial records and other key family matters, such as the will or trust documents, and how to contact the family attorney, accountant, etc.

First 60 Days

1. **Private Business**—If you own or co-own a private business, tell your spouse how to run it or sell it. Give an idea of its value (or who would know) and what steps you would suggest if they choose to sell it.

2. **Balance Sheet**—Update your personal balance sheet every year, or more often if you have large fluctuations. Let your spouse know where you keep a copy. If you hold illiquid investments, list

your contact people and their phone numbers. List your life insurance benefit on your balance sheet as a footnote so your spouse can see on page 1 how much there will be to work with.

3. **Rearrange Your Balance Sheet**—If you feel confident with this, describe in general terms what should be done with your assets (including insurance proceeds) and liabilities. Identify one general financial advisor to help your spouse with the big picture.

   Identify sub-advisors for special projects; i.e., "call our realtor friend John Doe to sell our vacant lot," etc. Here, you might want to give your spouse and designated advisor some personal experience guidelines like, "Keep at least 50% liquid, AA, or higher quality bonds; no second trust deeds," etc.

4. **Home Mortgages**—Ideally, your finances can be arranged to retire all of your debt. But be careful. Your spouse may never again be able to get a large mortgage (without your income). Consider this when advising your spouse on either paying it down or paying it off.

5. **Unfinished Business**—Tell your spouse how to settle any outstanding debts, money that's owed to you, problem investments or sticky personal issues that might confront the family.

6. **Lifestyle**—Knowing what your spouse will have in the way of assets and approximate income, give supportive suggestions on your thoughts about keeping the house, etc. If you don't know, just let her (his) advisors figure this out once they have rearranged the assets and established a budget.

Blessing

Close your letter with a personal note to your spouse and family. You might consider giving a blessing to possibly re-marry, or loving words of encouragement about the future. It doesn't have to be long and maudlin, just sincere.

This type of letter will give your spouse and immediate family a sensible heads-up and head start in getting accustomed to your permanent absence. It only takes an hour to compose and it should be updated every couple of years.

Besides being a foresighted and loving document, it also compels you to make sure your insurance and investments will provide adequate protection for your family.

Chapter 27

Enjoy Your Wealth!

AN UNSETTLING FEELING of "can't get no satisfaction" can be an unexpected fallout from your success when your dreams fall short of your money. In our youth, we all had dreams of a big house and a comfortable retirement. Those dreams today still keep most of America striving ahead.

However, at some point between $5 million, $10 million and $20 million, those dreams are more than fulfilled. Unless you have a celebrity or royalty lifestyle, you have more than enough to acquire the security, freedom and peace of mind your money can give you. You wonder, *What difference does it really make if I ever make another dime? What's next?*

Another success mode has absolutely nothing to do with what the money will be used for. That method is simply the score-keeping contest to the *game* of business. Making more money itself is the goal as opposed to having an end purpose for the money. These people thrive from winning the game and the challenge of the business. They are the "Type A" workaholics who cannot enjoy a vacation because they're wrapped too tightly into their work. They go nuts if they retire, and often work until they die. When asked how much is enough, they always reply, "A little bit more." Work is number one. Balance and solid family and personal relationships are often distant memories.

There are other stereotypes and most people don't fit neatly into any category. However, having worked with dozens of ultra-wealthy clients, let me share with you a story about one of the happiest and most fulfilled.

After one of our accounts sold his business for about $25 million, he placed $17 million in a private foundation (no tax). His goal was to make $100,000 per month off the $17 million so he could give anonymously to his favorite charities! Today, he lives very comfortably in a nice "tract" house and drives a modest American-made car. You would never pick him out in a crowd, and you'll never read about him in a magazine. But if you ever met him, you'd feel an aura of joy and fulfillment that's second to none. Since he spends his time looking for ways to help other people, he sleeps very well at night.

Too noble for you? Remember, you can't take it with you. It is more sensible all the way around to give it away while you're alive, and watch the good it can do in lieu of trying to make a statement after you're gone. The most satisfied wealthy people have a heartfelt purpose for their money that goes way beyond a comfortable lifestyle.

In Bob Buford's book *Half Time*, he proposes that satisfaction in the second half of your life comes from achieving significance—instead of success.

"Significance" is unique and different for each of us, but it is often askew from the world's view of success which you've already achieved. Again, I encourage you to dream bigger.

How would you like to leave your mark on the world? What injustice would you like to try and help correct? What legacy would you like to leave for those who will follow in your footprints?

A worthwhile but sobering exercise is to write your eulogy. If you died today, how would people remember you? If it's not a good read for you, consider using your resources to do something significant that will get people to keep an everlasting remembrance of your generosity.

Ideally, your talents, resources and personal passions can converge on a purpose for your funds beyond the lifestyle needs of your family.

If so, you too can truly experience and relish a personal joy and fulfillment that will be second to none!

Glossary

1031 Exchange—IRS Code 1031. A method of deferring capital gains tax by exchanging one property for another. You must use a third party "Accommodator" to hold your money after a sale and go into a new property within 180 days.

Absolute Performance—A specific positive return target, e.g., 10% regardless of the performance of the general markets. (See Relative Performance.)

Agency Paper—Securities issued by eight U.S. Government-sponsored entities and federally regulated institutions. Always AAA rated but not backed by the full faith and credit of the U.S. Government. Examples are Student Loan Marketing Association (SLMA) and Federal National Mortgage Association (FNMA), also known as FANNIE MAE.

Angel Investor—A private investor or group of private investors who invest in start-up companies, mostly high tech. Investors do their own due diligence and fully accept high risk to reward ratios. Total of "angel round" investment is usually under $1 million and seeds initial incubation of company.

Arbitrage—Buying something with a predetermined sales

price or strategy. A type of stock management technique of buying companies with announced takeovers and betting that the sales are consummated.

Asset Allocation—A strategic division of investment assets. Basic allocation is usually among stocks, bonds, real estate and private business to diversify and balance a portfolio. May also refer to deeper diversification within an asset class; e.g., big cap, small cap, foreign and hedged stock management allocations.

Basis Points—One-hundredth ($\frac{1}{100}$) of a percentage point. 30 basis points equals $\frac{30}{100}$ of 1%. If the long bond goes from 5.75% to 5.85%, it has moved 10 basis points.

Block Trades—A large quantity of stock or bonds traded. Generally 10,000+ shares of stock or $200,000+ of bonds. These trades are handled by the senior traders at a securities firm's trading desk.

Bogey—A predetermined absolute or relative return target number (remember the enemy targets in the movie *Top Gun*?). The bogey is a mutually-agreed performance number by which a manager will be judged.

Call Option—A contract that grants the right to buy a stock at a specific price for a specific number of shares by a certain date. Buying a call option is a bet that the stock will go up.

Capital Calls—Additional money (capital) needed for an investment, usually a Limited Partnership or LLC. May be planned or unplanned, mandatory or optional. Failure to pay results, at best, in dilution, or at worst, loss of entire investment.

Cashless Collar—A stock-hedging technique designed to freeze the approximate price of a security for a few days to a few months. Most often used to limit potential loss on a large concentrated stock holding.

Charitable Remainder Trust (CRT)—An estate planning trust where an asset or cash is irrevocably placed in a trust. Income is distributed to one or more individuals according to an actuarial table. The principal passes to one or more charities upon the death of the grantor.

Commercial Paper—Short-term unsecured obligations (loans) issued by banks and corporations. Nearly always backed by a bank line of credit and issued only by top-rated entities.

Cone—A chart pattern depicting the sharp price drop of a security or commodity after a steep run up (or price spike).

Crummy Notice—Also known as Notice to Beneficiaries of Addition\Gift to Trust. A letter or notice sent to the specific beneficiaries of an irrevocable trust that gives the beneficiary an amount of time they can withdraw their portion of the current gift. Usually funds are not withdrawn. But this vehicle is necessary for the gift to an irrevocable trust to be considered as a present-interest gift which qualifies for the $10,000 annual exclusion.

Dollar Cost Average—An investment technique to invest a set dollar amount at consistent time intervals, e.g, once a month. Fewer shares are purchased at higher prices and more shares at lower prices. The end result is an average price per share below the mean price.

Durable Power of Attorney for Health Care—A Power of Attorney for health care decisions if the person granting the power becomes incapacitated. This vehicle is a statutory power and may not be available in all states. However, where available, it generally is used in place of a Living Will since it is exercisable without court interference.

Durable Power of Attorney for Property Management— A Power of Attorney specifically for property and other asset management which remains in effect if the person granting the Power of Attorney becomes incapacitated. Depending on the provisions, it may either be effective immediately or only after the person becomes incapacitated.

Dynasty (Perpetual) Trust—An irrevocable trust designed to continue for more than one generation of beneficiaries— often up to 100 years.

Exchange Funds—A large stock portfolio that imitates the S&P 500. Composed of individuals depositing concentrated stock holdings into a managed account to achieve diversification without selling their holdings.

Family Limited Partnership—A Limited Partnership (LP) which is specifically drafted so that ownership of all interests in the LP remains with the family. Often used to obtain discounted valuation of assets. Then a transfer of LP interest percentage can be made to an Irrevocable Trust for benefit of children and/or their descendants.

Family Office—A large or small office staffed with professionals whose sole purpose is investing, managing and monitoring money for a wealthy family.

Foreign Asset Partnership—A trust in which a foreign trust company is the single Trustee or a co-Trustee. There are several countries that have established laws that are beneficial to such banking/trust purposes. Once the trust is established, assets are transferred to the foreign trust company as Trustee. This trust works best with specific types of assets only.

Going Naked—A risky and aggressive stock-option strategy to write options (calls or puts) without the underlying stock as collateral. Limited income with unlimited potential loss.

Grandchild Generation Skip Transfer Tax—An Irrevocable Trust which allows savings on estate taxes by passing assets to grandchild(ren) instead of children, thereby reducing the number of times the assets are subject to transfer tax. If drafted and used properly, it can be completed in connection with the lifetime generation-skipping transfer tax exemption.

Grantor—Also known as Trustor or Settlor. The individual or institution transferring the asset(s) to someone else, often a trust.

Hedge Funds—Aggressive stock (and sometimes commodities) management style with both long and short positions. Most hedge their positions from general market volatility.

Usual fee is 20% of the profits for management. Attracts the best managers and sophisticated investors.

Institutional Grade Property—Larger real estate properties with multiple tenants or a single high-quality "credit" tenant. Generally over $10 million and owned by (or built for sale to) an institutional buyer (like a pension fund or REIT).

IRR (Internal Rate of Return)—A mathematical calculation that compounds a given rate of return over a period of time. Considered the most accurate return measurement.

Irrevocable Life Insurance Trust—A trust whose terms cannot be changed in any way. The Trust holds life insurance, usually on the life of the Grantor(s) and is outside the Grantor's taxable estate. Frequently used to provide the beneficiaries with cash to purchase estate assets, thereby creating estate liquidity.

Jointly and Severally—A legal term that requires two or more parties to be "on the hook" for the full amount of a financial obligation.

Large-Cap—Publicly traded large-capitalization corporation. Generally over $1 billion in market capitalization.

Lead Advisor—An experienced investment advisor who is knowledgeable in all aspects of a portfolio and who is the point man for information on every investment. Like the head football coach is to the owner of the team.

Letter of Intent—Initial deal-term sheet. Non-binding, it precedes a formal purchase and sale agreement for a business or real estate transaction.

Limited Liability Company (LLC)—An ownership form often used to co-own real estate or business. Liability is limited to the investment amount regardless of management involvement.

Limited Partnership (LP)—Real estate or business ownership form consisting of a general partner (manager) with unlimited liability and investors with limited liability.

Liquid—That portion of a portfolio that can be turned into cash in a few days. Generally bonds, stock and short-term loans. The rest of the portfolio is *illiquid*.

Living Trust—Also known as a Revocable Trust or an Inter Vivos Trust. A trust in which terms can be amended or revoked in part or wholly while Grantor or surviving Grantor is living. It is used primarily to avoid probate proceedings and costs to preserve both spouses' Unified Credit Amounts and control disbursement of the estate.

Living Will—A Living Will is *not* a will at all. Instead, it's the name given the written directive to your physician authorizing the physician or named agent to take you off life-support systems. In many states, this document is not statutory and could be contested and/or reversed by the court.

Long Bond—30-year U.S. Government Treasury bond. Often watched as an indicator of interest rate changes.

Margin—Loans from a brokerage firm secured by deposited securities. Interest rates are below prime rate and repayment terms are flexible. May be used to purchase additional stock or withdraw cash.

Margin Call—A mandatory loan reduction due to the price reduction of the underlying securities collateral. Can be "met" with a deposit of cash, securities, or partial or full sale of collateral securities.

Money Market Fund (MMF)—An interest-earning cash substitute savings account (not FDIC insured) with fixed-principal pricing and variable income earned. Liquid in one day. Dividends, interest payments and deposits are automatically placed in money market funds at brokerage firms.

Municipal Bonds—Munis. Debt obligation of a state or local government entity. Interest payments are usually federally tax-free and state tax-free to in-state residents and are paid every six months.

Northwest Quadrant—Compass coordinates referring to a risk-reward chart comparing a stock portfolio's performance to the S&P 500. The Northwest Quadrant (upper left) is most desirable as it has better returns but less risk than the S&P 500 (usually the center axis of the chart).

Offering Memorandums—Also known as Offering Circulars. These are legal documents prepared by a manager or general partner of a potential investment that disclose required information about the investment. Includes detailed description of the use of proceeds, objectives, management control and risk. Designed to protect both management and investor by giving "full disclosure."

Omnibus Account—A custodial account at a brokerage firm that's used by money managers to coordinate multiple stock transactions and keep securities safe. Also helps simplify record keeping.

"Open if" Letter—In case of death, a letter to spouse with timely and practical financial and lifestyle suggestions.

OTC Special—A stock distribution technique used by large brokerage firms to sell a big block of stock. Usually priced between the bid and ask price and often used to sell insider positions.

Personal Investment Charter—A personal Mission Statement for your investments. Usually detailed with specific goals, objectives, targeted returns, risk tolerance and timetables.

Post-Closing Liability—Liability of the seller after the close of the sale of a business generally stemming from a misrepresentation or breach of warranty by the seller.

Pour-Over Will—A will that transfers assets that were in the person's estate at death to a pre-existing trust. It is a companion document to the Living Trust. It can also provide for documentation to the court regarding a person's desires for guardianship of any minor children.

Predetermined Stop Loss—A sell order, placed in advance, that limits your loss on a stock to a specific dollar or percentage amount if the stock goes down. Stop loss orders can be moved up, e.g. 15% below a recent high, to lock in gains should the stock later drop in price.

Prime Funds—Also known as Prime Rate Funds. A public or private mutual fund that buys short-term corporate loans from banks that pay interest at approximately the current prime rate. Has similar income to bond funds. Theoretically, the price of the funds should be stable even when interest rates rise.

Private Placement Memorandum (PPM)—See Offering Memorandums.

Put Option—A contract that grants the right to sell a stock at a specific price on a specified number of shares by a certain date. Buying a put option is a bet that the stock will go down.

Qualified Personal Residence Trust (QPRT)—A trust in the tax code which allows the Grantor to transfer ownership of primary residence and/or one vacation property in trust at a reduced value (determined by schedules and interest rates), frequently using the lifetime gifting exemption for this transfer of value. The trust has a term of years where it remains the property of the Grantor. Only at the end of the term and if the Grantor is still alive is the gift completed.

Real Estate Investment Trust (REIT)—Public or private company that manages a large portfolio of real estate for shareholders. Usually concentrated in a specific real estate segment like shopping centers, apartments, hotels, office buildings, etc.

Relative Performance—Portfolio return-measuring technique based on comparison to an appropriate index; e.g., small cap stock manager's returns would be measured as to their relative performance (better or worse than) versus the Russell 2000 Index returns.

Representations and Warranties—Assurances given (primarily by seller) in a business acquisition that the description of the business is true in all material aspects.

Restricted Stock—Also known as Lettered Stock. Usually owned by an original investor or insider, this stock is not freely saleable and can only be sold according to volume and time restrictions. Sometimes referred to as 144 or 145 Stock (rule numbers). Often cannot be sold for 6 months after an IPO and in limited amounts during months 6 through 24.

Revocable Living Trust—See Living Trust.

Round Trip—A completed project or investment, e.g., money raised to buy land, building constructed, building leased up and sold and the final proceeds distributed to the investors. Used to evaluate performance of past investments.

Selling Memorandum—See Offering Memorandums.

Selling Team—The group of brokers dedicated to distributing (selling) a public or private security to their clients.

Spike—A sharp rise in the price of a security or commodity. It is often followed by a price drop. See *Cone*.

Stock Hedging—A stock management technique used to limit the volatility or downside risk of a given security without selling it. It's like buying insurance against a price decline.

Tenants-in-Common—The simplest co-ownership of an asset. Each investor owns an undivided pro-rata share of the investment and all have to agree to sell, finance, etc.

Term Insurance—Term life insurance is written for a specific period (term) that provides for an amount of money to be paid to beneficiaries if the insured party dies. No cash build up or permanent coverage.

Time Value of Money—A mathematical calculation that compounds a rate of return (or inflation) over a period of years. If you invest $10,000 per year for 10 years and earn 10% per year, the 10-year future value will be $175,311 from compounding.

Trust Deeds—A legal document securing real property as collateral for a loan. It requires a third party (Trustee) to facilitate title transfer.

Uniform Gift to Minors (UGMA)—A simple account established to transfer cash or assets to minors without a formal trust. An adult custodian oversees the account until the minor reaches ages 18 or 21, depending on the state.

Usury Laws—State laws limiting excessive interest charged on loans.

Valuation Multiplier—A figure used to evaluate a purchase price of a company for sale. It is derived by dividing 100% by the desired rate of return, e.g., 100%/20% = 5, the Valuation Multiplier. The earnings of the company to be acquired are then multiplied by the multiplier to arrive at the proposed purchase price of the company.

Venture Capital Fund—Private pool of capital generated by investors that invests in a group of non-public companies. VC Funds are risky, volatile, illiquid and based on the assumption that most investments will fail. But a few make 50–100 times returns and provide a 30%–50% IRR.

Viatical—An investment in the discounted purchase of the death benefit from an insurance policy based on the life of a terminally ill patient.

Wealth Replacement Insurance—Used in combination with a gift to charity (as in CRTs) to provide an equal benefit to the heirs.

Wire House—A large securities brokerage firm, e.g., Merrill Lynch. Originally referred to the order transmission "wire" used to place trades.

Working a Stock—When an institutional stock trader strategically buys or sells a stock over a period of time to achieve the best execution price.

Index